From Chaos to Control: Building a Balanced, Stress-Free Financial Life

About Money Prep Academy

Money Prep Academy, based in the heart of Glastonbury, Somerset, UK, is committed to delivering practical and accessible financial education and is specialized in equipping individuals and families with the tools they need to take control of their financial futures. From building emergency funds to planning for major life goals like buying a home or saving for retirement, our mission is to simplify personal finance and empower people to achieve financial stability and success.

Our website,

ww.moneyprepacademy.co.uk,

serves as a resource hub where you can find valuable tips, guides, and online courses tailored to all stages of your financial journey.

Disclaimer:

The information provided in this book, including any recommendations of tools, resources, or books, is for general informational and educational purposes only.

Money Prep Academy® Ltd and the author, **Alina Salabin**, are not affiliated with any of the products, companies, or authors mentioned in this book, and we do not receive any financial compensation for their inclusion. The recommendations are based solely on our independent assessment and should not be construed as endorsements.

While we strive to provide accurate and up-to-date information, personal finance is a complex subject, and every individual's financial situation is unique. The content in this book does not constitute financial, legal, or tax advice. We encourage readers to consult with another qualified professional for advice tailored to their specific circumstances.

Money Prep Academy® Ltd *and the author cannot be held responsible for any actions taken based on the information provided in this book, nor for any losses, legal liabilities, or other consequences that may result. By using the information in this book, you agree that you are solely responsible for your financial decisions.*

From Chaos to Control: Building a Balanced, Stress-Free Financial Life

Creating a Safety Net, Even When Times Are Tough

For many people, the idea of saving money while living pay cheque to pay cheque feels like a distant dream. When you're in survival mode, struggling just to cover rent, groceries, and bills, talking about savings can feel overwhelming or even impossible. But here's the truth: **it's not about how much you save at once; it's about the habit of saving**, even in small amounts.

We often think of savings as something only for those who have extra income, but building financial security is about **small, steady steps**, not big leaps. The key is to start with what you have, no matter how little that might be.

I want to show you how to shift your mindset and start viewing savings as a long-term tool, even when money is tight. It's about thinking differently and finding ways to make saving part of your routine, no matter how small the amounts.

Let's start with this simple concept: **Tiny Savings are Powerful!** When you're living pay cheque to pay cheque, the idea of setting aside large chunks of money is unrealistic. But what if you could save just £1 or £5 here and there?

It may not seem like much, but even tiny savings can have a big impact over time. Small amounts really do add up, and here's why saving, even a few pounds, is so powerful. First, it helps you build a habit. The more often you save, no matter how small the amount, the more it becomes part of your routine. It's not about how much you save but about creating the habit of saving regularly, **it trains your mind** to think about setting money aside.

As you start to see those savings grow, even if it's just £5 turning into £50 or £100, it builds momentum. You'll feel encouraged to keep going because that's money you didn't have before, and every bit counts. Most importantly, saving, even just a little, gives you a sense of control over your finances.

Making the choice to save, even when it's tough, shows that you have the power to change your situation. Little by little, it makes a real difference. We name this at Money Prep Academy®: "One Penny at a Time".

Breaking the Cycle: You Can Do This!

Living pay cheque to pay cheque can feel like you're stuck in a never-ending cycle, where every pound is already gone before it even hits your account. I understand, it feels like there's just never enough money when you're in survival mode. But here's the good news: **it is possible to break this cycle**, even if it takes time and small steps.

It will start eventually by shifting your mindset. Instead of thinking, "I can't afford to save," try asking yourself, "How can I save, even just a little?". This small shift helps you spot opportunities to save, no matter how tight things feel.

Then, **start with micro-savings**. It might be just £1, £2, or £5 - maybe it's spare change from a grocery trip or a couple of pounds you saved by skipping that coffee.

These tiny amounts can be set aside in a jar or transferred to a separate savings account, and over time, they do add up.

If possible, **automate what you can**. Even if it's just £10 a month, set up an automatic transfer to your savings account. Automation takes the decision-making out of the equation and helps you build that savings cushion without thinking about it, and you'll be surprised at how it grows. Anyway, if you automate it will be convenient, but you will not train your brain to save. To train yourself you must do it on a regulate basis.

When thinking about savings one of the most helpful steps is to **create a bare-bones emergency fund**. If you don't have any savings yet, aim for just £100 to start. That small buffer can cover unexpected costs without relying on credit or on borrowing from dear ones for once. Once you reach £100 celebrate, and then go again and stretch your goal to £200, and then go on. Each step gives you more breathing room.

Finally, **look for small wins**. Sometimes, even when it feels like there's no wiggle room, a small windfall comes your way, maybe a tax rebate, a birthday gift, or selling something you no longer need. Whenever you get a little extra, try to put at least part of it into your savings instead of spending it all. These small actions, over time, can help you slowly but surely break the cycle.

From Chaos to Control: Building a Balanced, Stress-Free Financial Life

How to Find Room for Savings When There's "No Room"

You might be thinking, "There's no room in my budget to save." And that's totally understandable. But sometimes, a few small changes can free up more cash than you'd expect. One of the first things you can try is **tracking every pound** you spend for a week or even a month. Simply paying attention to where your money is going can help you spot those little expenses you didn't even realize were adding up, like takeout, online subscriptions, or small impulse purchases. Once you see it all laid out, it's easier to adjust.

Another idea is to **challenge yourself** with a "no-spend weekend" or even a week where you only spend on essentials. Pressing pause on extra spending, even for a few days, can show you how much you're able to save. It's a fun experiment that often surprises people when they realize how much they can keep in their pocket by cutting out unnecessary purchases for a short time.

You can also **downsize temporarily**. Look at your services or subscriptions, could you cancel or pause one for a month or two and direct that money toward savings instead? Or maybe you could negotiate a lower utility bill or switch to a cheaper phone plan.

These small changes don't have to be forever, just long enough to help you start building a cushion.

And finally, **celebrate the small wins**. Did you managed to save £10 this month? That's a victory! Add it to your emergency fund and give yourself credit for making progress. Little by little, these wins add up and help you build the habit of saving.

I remember the exact opposite of this feeling now. Back, *"on my salad days"* how a very smart person said once, when my budget was tight, I'd often find myself thinking, *"Oh, it's just £8,"* whether it was a toy for the kids or a new cosmetic I didn't really need. I'd convince myself that these little purchases wouldn't affect my month, and in the moment, it felt harmless. But, one small purchase led to another, and before I knew it, those *"just a few pounds"* here and there added up, eating away at my budget in a big, big way.

Looking back, *it was madness!* I spent money on things that weren't even necessary, like toys my children barely played with or beauty products that ended up collecting dust. At the end of the day, none of those purchases mattered. What I realize now is how much I could have saved for what I like to call my "**important savings**" account. The power of reflection is amazing, when you finally see the amount of waste, you realize how much more you could have done for your financial health. It's a valuable lesson, and one I wish I had learned sooner! But better late than never, right?

The Long Game: Progress Over Perfection

Saving while living pay cheque to pay cheque won't be easy, and it won't happen overnight. But the goal is **progress, not perfection**. Life might throw curveballs, sometimes curves, and sometimes balls, and some months you may not be able to save at all. That's okay, what matters is that you keep trying.

Every step you take toward saving, no matter how small, is a step toward financial security. Building savings is about creating a safety net for the future, a net that grows stronger each time you add to it.

It will take time, but that's okay, because over time, you'll find that saving (even when it feels impossible) helps you gain control over your finances and your life. You will have more control over your choices.

From Chaos to Control: Building a Balanced, Stress-Free Financial Life

You Deserve Financial Peace

No matter where you are on your financial journey, you deserve to have peace of mind. You deserve to live without constantly worrying about the next unexpected bill or how you'll make it to the next pay cheque. Savings, even small amounts, give you that peace of mind, and building the habit of saving it will train your mind to always have a plan. It will help you a lot on the long run.

So, if you've ever told yourself that saving is impossible, that it's only for people who already have extra, remember this: **you can start today, with what you have, where you are**. Every pound you save is a step toward financial stability and a future where you're in control.

Chapter 1: The Foundation

Managing money might seem like a huge task, but don't worry, you're not alone on this journey. In this book we'll explore practical ways to bring your finances under control. This isn't just about crunching numbers or cutting costs, it's about turning financial chaos into calm and finding peace of mind in your financial future.

Think of this process as an adventure, one that you're taking as a family. Like any journey, there will be ups and downs, but there is a lesson in this book and if learned it will set you up for success, one small step at a time.

You'll not only learn how to manage your money smartly, but also how to have fun along the way, building strong habits that lead to financial security. Managing money can feel overwhelming, but you are not the only one in facing financial chaos. Whether it's living pay cheque to pay cheque (struggling to save for the future, or simply not having a plan and just wasting all your money) many of us find ourselves caught in cycles that feel impossible to break. The good news?

You can move from chaos to control, and this book will guide you.

Think of this journey as a family adventure. You'll read about other families, who face different financial struggles but share the same goal, to gain financial peace of mind.

Throughout the book, we'll follow their journeys as they move from chaos to a place of financial stability and security.

Meet the Johnson Family: Balancing Spending and Saving

The Johnson family is a family of four and lives on an average family income. They are Sarah, James, and their two kids, Max and Emily. On the surface, they seem to be doing okay. Both Sarah and James have steady jobs, but behind closed doors, their finances are a source of stress. Sarah loves treating the kids and grabbing coffee on the way to work. She thinks, "What's the harm in a little treat here and there?" But those small purchases add up.

James, on the other hand, is focused on saving. He's been trying to build up an emergency fund for years, but every time they make progress, something unexpected happens. Maybe it's a school event that needs paying for, or the car breaks down. And while they've tried to sit down and budget, it never seems to stick.

Their financial chaos stems from one key issue: balance. They know they need to save for the future, but living for today always seems to take priority.

Reflection Questions:

Are you in a constant battle between saving and spending? How often do small, everyday purchases add up without you realizing it, and how could understanding their impact help you find a better balance?

Does the pressure of unexpected expenses throw off your financial goals? How would having even a small emergency fund reduce your stress and give you more control over these situations?

How could balancing short-term wants with long-term needs bring peace to your family? What would it feel like to have financial security without feeling deprived today?

From Chaos to Control: Building a Balanced, Stress-Free Financial Life

What does financial peace of mind mean to you? Imagine a life without financial stress, what would change, and what could that allow you to do?

Do you see your spending habits clearly, or are there areas you might be overlooking? Could tracking your spending for a week or a month help you understand where your money is going?

What are your family's financial priorities? Have you discussed these as a family, and are you all on the same page about what matters most for your financial future?

As I reflect on these questions, I remember being in that constant tug-of-war between wanting to enjoy today and worrying about tomorrow. Well, the truth is many times I did not cared about tomorrow. I was and I still am in many ways like Sarah. I love buying stuff for my kids. The truth is, finding the right balance is key. There's no magic formula, but small steps, clear priorities, and honest conversations about money can make all the difference.

It's not about perfection, it's about making progress and finding peace in the process. The Johnson family, like so many others, are willing to take that first step, and you can too. With each reflection we can gain clarity, a perspective, and let`s hope that, we gain a motivation to change what we dislike.

We're often really good at spending for others, aren't we? When we see something that we like, we tell ourselves, "Oh, this is only £8," and we buy it, not because we need it, but because we want it in that moment. The problem? It doesn't come out of our "joy fund" or any planned budget. It's like we're saving for someone else, but never ourselves.

The truth is, if we were to count these small purchases, just 10 like that £8, each month, suddenly it's £80 that could have gone into our savings. It's amazing how these amounts build up when we're not paying attention.

That's why it's so helpful to have **separate accounts** for our main expenses.

When we can clearly see where our money is going, it becomes much easier to notice where things are going wrong and take action to fix it.

Meet the Walker Family: The Single Parent Balancing Act

Lisa Walker is a single mom raising her two children, Jake and Chloe. Lisa works full-time as a nurse and does everything she can to give her kids a good life. But between rent, groceries, school supplies, and other expenses, there's barely anything left at the end of the month.

Lisa's financial chaos comes from living pay cheque to pay cheque. She dreams of giving her children a better future, maybe even saving for university expenses, but there's simply no extra money for saving. Each month is a new struggle, and Lisa worries about what might happen if something goes wrong. She doesn't have an emergency fund, and even a small, unexpected bill could push her into debt.

What makes it harder is the emotional toll. Lisa is constantly juggling the roles of mom, provider, and problem-solver. She knows she needs a plan, but where to start?

Reflection Questions:

Do you feel like you're always one emergency away from financial disaster? How would your life change if you had a small buffer in place to handle those unexpected expenses?

How could building a safety net help you feel more secure about the future? Imagine the relief of knowing that even if something goes wrong, you have a cushion to protect you.

What steps can you take to create some breathing room in your budget? Could small adjustments, like cutting unnecessary expenses or setting aside even tiny amounts, help you build that safety net over time?

Reflecting on these questions, I'm reminded of my own experiences growing up in a single-parent household. My mother was incredible, working tirelessly to provide for me while navigating the financial pressures of raising a child alone. There were times when it felt like we were always on the edge, just **one emergency away from financial disaster**. But her resilience taught me the value of creating some form of security, no matter how small it seemed at the time.

Like Lisa from the Walker family, many single parents face that overwhelming pressure of being both provider and protector. It's exhausting, and the emotional toll is real. But even in those moments of uncertainty, taking small steps to build a safety net can make all the difference. It doesn't happen overnight, but as I've learned through my own journey, **progress is key**. Every small adjustment, whether it's finding a few pounds to set aside or cutting out an unnecessary expense, can bring you closer to feeling more in control of your financial future.

It's not about perfection, but about giving yourself the **peace of mind** that you and your family are going to be okay, one step at a time, if you do something about it.

Meet the Martin Family: The Child-Free Couple with Big Dreams

Chloe and David Martin are in their late 30s. They've been married for 10 years and don't have children. Instead, they have big dreams, specifically, starting their own tech business. David is a software developer with a passion for building apps, and Chloe works in marketing, so they feel like they have the perfect combination of skills to succeed. The problem? They don't have the capital to get started.

Chloe and David's financial chaos comes from their ambitious dreams clashing with reality. They've saved some money over the years, but not nearly enough to launch their business. Every time they think about taking the plunge, they realize how much more they need, whether it's for software, marketing, or just keeping themselves afloat until the business takes off.

Their dream of entrepreneurship often feels out of reach, and they're not sure how to move from where they are now to building the life and business they've envisioned. The pressure of wanting to succeed but not having the resources creates a constant stress, and they feel stuck.

From Chaos to Control: Building a Balanced, Stress-Free Financial Life

Reflection Questions:

Do you have big dreams but feel like the financial means to achieve them are far away? What would it take to break down that big goal into smaller, more manageable steps, so it doesn't feel so overwhelming?

How could building a solid financial foundation make your dream more achievable? Imagine having a plan in place that not only protects your day-to-day finances but also makes space for you to take the risks needed to chase your dreams.

Are there small steps you can take now to begin moving toward your goal? Even if the final goal feels distant, what actions could you take today, this week, or this month that would inch you closer to where you want to be?

Reading Chloe and David's story brings me back to the time when I was at university. That's when I had the biggest, boldest dreams, ideas that felt groundbreaking, full of potential, and ready to change the world. And back then, it felt like nothing could stop me. The enthusiasm was real, but over time, without structure or a plan, those dreams can start to feel more and more distant. That's the reality for so many of us.

We have incredible ideas, full of passion, but without a financial plan or action steps, the dream starts to drift further away. The truth is, no matter how exciting your vision is, if you can't afford to pursue it, frustration builds. And that's what happened to me too when dreams seemed just out of reach because I hadn't laid the foundation.

But here's what I learned, and what Chloe and David can still do: **Structure is key**. Break down the dream into manageable pieces. Focus on small, consistent actions that can build toward the bigger goal. When you combine ambition with a plan, even if it takes time, you start to regain control and confidence. Your dreams don't have to fade away; they just need a structure to grow within. And every step you take toward that structure brings you one step closer to making it a reality.

Meet the Castillo Family: The Family Business Under Stress

The Castillos, Maria and Jorge, run a small family business, a bakery that has been in the family for generations. While their business keeps them busy, it's also a source of constant stress. Every bit of profit they make goes directly to their personal income, and they struggle to reinvest in the business to help it grow.

Maria and Jorge's financial chaos is rooted in their inability to separate their personal and business finances. They often feel like they're chasing their tails, one month, they need money to cover family expenses, and the next, they need to pay for new bakery equipment. They've never had the chance to build a financial cushion for their business, and they often find themselves dipping into credit lines to stay afloat.

The stress of balancing family needs with business expenses has become overwhelming. They both know they need to make a change, but the question is, how do they fix things when they feel like they're barely keeping their heads above water?

Reflection Questions:

Are you struggling to balance personal and business finances? How often do you find that the money meant for business reinvestment gets used to cover personal expenses?

Does your business income feel like it's disappearing into your family's needs, leaving little room for growth? How would separating your personal and business finances help you create a clearer path forward for both?

What steps can you take to create a financial cushion for your business? How could prioritizing reinvestment in the business relieve some of the stress and provide more stability for your family in the long run?

The Castillos' story brings to mind another couple I once knew who faced a similar struggle. They were an incredible family, with the father working tirelessly, often to the point of physical exhaustion. He was running a successful business that brought in £6,000 to £7,000 a month, but they were constantly living on the edge, financially. Despite the hard work and decent earnings, they never seemed to have enough to reinvest in their business or even make the necessary purchases, like hiring help or buying a new van for their business.

The reason? Every bit of their business income was drained into covering family expenses, leaving nothing for the business itself. They found themselves stuck in a vicious cycle, no money to grow the business, and the personal finances consumed whatever little was left. Month after month, they'd end up back at square one, despite their hard work. The stress this created, both financially and emotionally, was overwhelming.

What I learned from their situation, and what the Castillos need to realize, is that **separating personal and business finances is crucial**. When your business money is constantly mixed with your personal expenses, it's impossible to see where you're really at, or to invest in the future growth of your business. It's not an easy shift to make, especially when you're already struggling to stay afloat, but it's the key to creating a more stable, sustainable future.

Why Reflecting on the Chaos Matters

Now that we've met these families, it's important to understand why they're all facing chaos in their financial lives. For the Johnsons, it's about balance. For Lisa Walker, it's the struggle of managing on a single income. For the Martins, it's figuring out how to fund their dreams. And for the Castillos, it's finding a way to make both their family and business thrive without sacrificing one for the other.

These stories reflect the reality that many families face, there are different types of financial chaos, but the common thread is that none of these families has a solid financial plan.

Whether it's about building savings, managing cash flow, or pursuing long-term goals, they all need to take a step back, assess their situation, and create a roadmap that helps them move forward.

What Being "Smart" with Money Really Means

Being smart with money isn't just about making more or cutting expenses. It's about creating a plan that works for you. It's about understanding your current financial habits, taking control of your income, and building a future that supports your goals, whether it's buying a house, starting a business, or simply having the peace of mind that comes from knowing you're financially secure.

This book will guide you through practical steps to regain control of your finances and build a more secure future. You'll discover how to **build a budget** that fits your unique situation. Whether you're balancing family expenses, a small business, or personal goals, you'll learn how to manage your money in a way that works for you, not against you.

You will also learn how to **create an emergency fund** to give yourself a cushion when life throws you down. This is your safety net, a fund that protects you whether it's an emergency medical bill, a car repair, or something else entirely.

You will learn some things about how to **save for your future**, whether that means setting aside money for your children's education, funding your dream business, or planning for your retirement. Saving is about taking control of tomorrow, so you can build toward something bigger.

And my favourite part is that we will **explore passive income** ideas that allow your money to work for you, even when you're not working. Whether it's investing, creating a side income, or using your existing skills in a new way, we'll look at ways to help you generate income that doesn't rely on your daily effort.

What's Next?

Now that we've introduced these families and their struggles, we'll dive deeper into understanding the financial chaos that holds them back, and how you can start identifying the issues in your own financial life. In the next chapter, we'll explore why it's important to sit down, assess the situation, and begin creating a plan for improvement.

By the end of this journey, you'll have the tools to move from chaos to control, just like these families will have. So, let's start, shall we?

Chapter 2: Starting with Chaos: Identifying the Problem

Financial chaos doesn't just appear out of nowhere. It creeps in slowly, through unplanned expenses, impulse purchases, or simply not having a clear idea of where your money is going. The truth is, we all experience financial chaos at some point in our lives. It's how we deal with it that makes the difference between constantly feeling stressed and gaining control over our financial future.

In this chapter, we'll revisit our four families, each of them dealing with their own version of financial chaos. They all know that things aren't quite right, but they've never sat down to fully reflect on their situation. Let's follow them as they begin to identify the problem and take the first steps toward their financial clarity.

The Johnson Family: Balancing Spending and Saving

When we last met the Johnsons, they were struggling to balance their short-term desires and long-term needs. Sarah's impulse spending and James' frustration with their inability to save created tension, and they often felt like they were taking one step forward, two steps back. Now, they're finally sitting down to take a hard look at their finances.

Reflection:

James pulls up their bank statements from the past few months and starts highlighting all the unplanned expenses, online shopping, dining out, and small impulse buys. The total adds up faster than they expected. Sarah is shocked at how much they've spent without really noticing. They are starting initially to fight, but at the end of the day together they are starting to realize that while they've been trying to save, they haven't been clear about their priorities.

They've never had a solid budget, and as a result, their money has been slipping through the cracks.

Both Sarah and James finally agree: if they don't make some changes soon, their financial chaos will keep getting worse.

What They Learned:
- They need to stop living month to month without a clear plan.
- They have to find a balance between enjoying life now and saving for the future.
- Small impulse purchases add up quickly and throw off their ability to save.

Action Step for the Johnsons:
James and Sarah decide to track their spending for the next month and build a simple budget. They'll focus on prioritizing savings while still leaving room for small treats, without letting those treats derail their goals.
It is initially hard to do, but not impossible, let`s hope they will manage it. What is important is that they have now the same vision.

The Walker Family: Breaking the Pay cheque to Pay cheque Cycle

For Lisa Walker, the chaos comes from constantly living pay cheque to pay cheque. She works hard as a single mom, but the money always seems to run out before the month is over. She's stressed, exhausted, and worried about what will happen if an emergency arises. Today, Lisa is sitting down to take a closer look at her finances.

Reflection:

Lisa lays out all her bills, rent, groceries, childcare, utilities, and realizes that while she's covering the basics, there's no room for anything else. Every time she gets a little ahead, something unexpected happens: the car breaks down, Jake needs new school supplies, or Chloe's after-school program requires a new fee.

With no emergency fund, Lisa has to dip into her already stretched pay cheque to cover these expenses, leaving her even more stressed.

She knows she needs to start saving, but the problem is: where does the money come from?

What She Learned:

- Living pay cheque to pay cheque means there's no room for unexpected expenses, which causes constant stress.
- She needs to build an emergency fund, but first, she has to find a way to create some breathing room in her budget.
- Without a clear plan, she'll continue to feel stuck, constantly treading water.

Action Step for Lisa:

Lisa decides to start small. She'll aim to save just £20 from each pay cheque to begin building a tiny emergency fund. Even though it feels like a small step, it gives her a sense of control. She also looks at areas where she might cut back, like reducing grocery costs or finding free activities for the kids, to free up a little more money.

The Martin Family: Bridging the Gap Between Dreams and Reality

Chloe and David Martin have big dreams. They want to start a tech business, but their reality is that they don't have enough saved to make it happen. Every time they make a little progress, something seems to get in the way, whether it's unexpected expenses or the cost of maintaining their current lifestyle. They're starting to wonder if their dream will ever become a reality.

Reflection:

Chloe and David decide to take a hard look at their financial picture. They sit down together and list out their income, expenses, and how much they've managed to save so far.

While they've done a decent job of setting aside money, they realize their savings are being eaten away by unexpected costs, car repairs, medical bills, and even social events. Every time they feel like they're making progress, something derails them.

They realize they've been focused on their dream without laying a strong enough financial foundation. It's not just about saving for the business; it's about ensuring they're financially stable in the present so they can take calculated risks in the future.

What They Learned:
- They've been so focused on their big goal that they haven't prioritized building a financial cushion for day-to-day expenses.
- They need to slow down and start building an emergency fund that will protect them from financial setbacks.
- It's okay to have big dreams, but those dreams need to be built on a solid financial foundation.

Action Step for the Martins:
Chloe and David agree to hit pause on their business savings for a few months. Instead, they'll focus on building an emergency fund that will give them more stability.

Once they've built that cushion, they'll return to saving for their business dream with more confidence.

The Castillo Family: The Struggle of Business and Personal Finances

Carlos and Maria Castillo are passionate about their family-run bakery. It's their pride and joy, but financially, it's a constant struggle. The bakery's profits cover their family's personal expenses, leaving little to reinvest in the business. They know they need to grow the business to make it more profitable, but they never have enough funds to reinvest.

Reflection:

Carlos and Maria sit down to review their financials, both personal and business. As they go through the numbers, it becomes clear that they've been treating the business's profits as their personal income, which means the bakery never has a chance to grow.

Without reinvestment, the bakery struggles to keep up with competition, but without taking some of the profits home, they can't cover their family's needs.

They realize they're stuck in a cycle of consuming the business's profits without ever investing in its future.

It's a tough situation, but they know they need to make some changes if they want both their business and their family to thrive.

What They Learned:
- By treating the business's profits as their personal income, they've limited the bakery's potential for growth.
- They need to create clear boundaries between personal and business finances.
- Without reinvesting in the business, they'll continue to struggle to make ends meet both personally and professionally.

Action Step for the Castillos:
Carlos and Maria decide to set aside a small percentage of the business's profits each month to reinvest in the bakery, whether it's for new equipment, marketing, or improvements. At the same time, they'll look for ways to reduce their personal expenses to free up more of the business's income for growth.

Seeing the Bigger Picture: Why We Need a Plan

All of these families have one thing in common: **financial chaos.** But what they're beginning to understand is that chaos doesn't have to last forever. By reflecting on their situations and understanding where things have gone wrong, they're taking the first step toward regaining control.

The Johnsons are learning to balance their spending and savings. Lisa is starting to break free from the payslip-to-payslip cycle. The Martins are pausing to build a stronger foundation before chasing their big dreams. And the Castillos are realizing they need to invest in both their business and their family.

This chapter isn't just about identifying the problem, it's about realizing that a plan can turn chaos into clarity. With each step, they're embracing the power of small, intentional changes, knowing that even small actions can lead to a significant transformation. Financial chaos may be where they started, but it's not where they have to stay.

What's Next? Creating a Roadmap for Success

Now that we've reflected on the chaos, it's time to start building a plan. In the next chapter, we'll guide these families - and you - through the process of creating a simple, realistic budget. This budget will be your roadmap, helping you prioritize savings, manage expenses, and build a more secure tomorrow.

Reflection Questions:
1. Which family's financial situation resonates most with you? Why?
2. What areas of your financial life feel the most chaotic right now?
3. Are you ready to take the next step in creating a financial plan?

Use the next pages if you need to reflect in writing at these questions, add more of you have, "speak" your mind and try to visualise what you want for your future.

From Chaos to Control: Building a Balanced, Stress-Free Financial Life

From Chaos to Control: Building a Balanced, Stress-Free Financial Life

Chapter 3: Building a Family Budget that Works

Creating a budget can feel daunting, but the truth is, a good budget isn't about restriction, it's about freedom. By giving every pound a purpose, you stop wondering where your money went and start deciding where it should go.

A well-thought-out budget gives you the power to prioritize what matters most, whether it's saving for the future, building an emergency fund, or simply enjoying life without financial stress.

In this chapter, we'll follow our four families as they build their own budgets. Each family has a unique situation, but they all share the same goal: to bring order to their finances and stop living in chaos.

By doing so, they're discovering that budgeting isn't just a financial tool, it's a way to regain control, find peace, and make choices that align with their values and long-term goals.

The Johnson Family: Finding Balance Between Saving and Spending

For the Johnsons, building a budget is about finding balance. Sarah and James know they need to save for the future, but they also want to enjoy life in the present. After reflecting on their financial chaos, they're ready to create a budget that works for both of them, one that allows them to save while still leaving room for small indulgences.

Step 1: Track Your Income and Expenses

James and Sarah start by gathering all their bank statements and listing out their income and expenses. They realize they've been underestimating how much they spend on things like dining out, coffee runs, and impulse purchases for the kids.

By tracking their expenses, they can see where their money is really going.

Step 2: Prioritize Savings

They both agree that saving is their priority. They decide to set up an automatic transfer into a savings account every month, this way, they save before they even have the chance to spend. They start small, transferring £150 a month into their emergency fund, with a goal of building up three months' worth of living expenses over time.

Step 3: Create a "Fun Money" Category

To keep the budget from feeling restrictive, they set aside £120 a month as "fun money" for dining out, entertainment, and small treats. This allows Sarah to indulge without feeling guilty, while keeping James confident that their savings are on track.

Their Budget at a Glance:
- **Income:** £4,000 (combined)
- **Essentials:** £2,500 (rent, groceries, bills)
- **Savings:** £150 (emergency fund)
- **Debt Repayment:** £250 (car loan, credit card)
- **Fun Money:** £120

Reflection:

By creating a budget that balances their needs and wants, Sarah and James feel more in control. They're no longer stressed about spending, and they know that their savings are growing each month.

The Walker Family: Breaking Free from Pay cheque-to-Pay cheque

For Lisa Walker, the goal is to break free from the pay cheque-to-pay cheque cycle. She knows she needs to start saving, but it feels impossible with her tight budget. Building a budget for Lisa means finding a way to create a small buffer that gives her some breathing room.

Step 1: List Income and Expenses

Lisa starts by listing her income and monthly expenses. Her rent, utilities, and childcare take up most of her pay cheque, and she realizes she's been spending more than she thought on groceries and small, everyday purchases for her kids.

Step 2: Find Areas to Cut Back

With no obvious savings to tap into, Lisa looks for areas to cut back. She decides to trim her grocery bill by meal planning and shopping sales.

She also cancels a couple of subscriptions services that she and the kids rarely use, saving an extra £15 a month. These small changes free up £50 a month that she can put into savings.

Step 3: Build a Small Emergency Fund

Lisa starts small, putting £50 a month into a savings account. It doesn't feel like much, but it's a start, and it gives her peace of mind knowing she's building a cushion for unexpected expenses.

Her Budget at a Glance:
- **Income:** £2,500
- **Essentials:** £1,800 (rent, childcare, bills)
- **Savings:** £50 (emergency fund)
- **Debt Repayment:** £100 (credit card)
- **Remaining:** £550 (groceries, transport, personal expenses)

Reflection:
Even though Lisa's budget is tight, she feels empowered by the changes she's made. She's starting to save for the first time, and the small buffer she's building gives her hope.

Each week, as she watches her savings grow bit by bit, she's gaining a sense of control she never thought possible. What was once overwhelming now feels manageable, and her confidence is rising. The process isn't just about numbers, it's about knowing she has the power to improve her situation, even in small, steady steps forward.

The Martin Family: Saving for Big Dreams

Chloe and David Martin have big ambitions, they want to save enough to start their tech business. But first, they need to create a budget that allows them to save consistently, while also covering their living expenses and building a safety net for unexpected costs.

Step 1: Calculate Their Expenses

Chloe and David start by calculating their monthly expenses. They realize that while they've been good at saving for their business, they've neglected their personal savings. Every time an unexpected expense comes up, they dip into their business fund, slowing down their progress.

Step 2: Separate Personal and Business Savings

They decide to create two separate savings accounts - one for their business and one for personal emergencies. They agree to save £300 a month for their business, while setting aside £200 a month in their personal emergency fund. This way, they won't have to touch their business savings when personal expenses arise.

Step 3: Adjust Their Lifestyle

To make this work, they agree to cut back on unnecessary expenses, like dining out and expensive hobbies. It's a small sacrifice, but one that will help them reach their goals faster.

Their Budget at a Glance:
- **Income:** £5,000 (combined)
- **Essentials:** £2,200 (rent, bills, groceries)
- **Business Savings:** £300
- **Personal Savings:** £200 (emergency fund)
- **Fun Money:** £100
- **Debt Repayment:** £200 (student loans)

Reflection:

By separating their business and personal finances, Chloe and David are finally making progress toward their dream. They feel confident that they can handle some personal emergencies without derailing their business goals. Now, with clearer boundaries, they no longer feel the constant pressure of one financial aspect draining the other. They can focus on growing their business, knowing that their personal needs are covered. This newfound balance gives them peace of mind and the motivation to keep moving forward, trusting that they are building a stronger future for themselves, together.

The Castillo Family: Balancing Business and Family

For the Castillo family, the biggest challenge is balancing the needs of their family with the needs of their bakery. They've been treating the bakery's profits as personal income, leaving little to reinvest in the business.

Now, they're building a budget that allows them to grow the bakery while still covering their family's expenses.

Step 1: Track Business and Personal Income

Maria and Carlos sit down and list their business income and personal expenses. They realize that by treating the business's profits as personal income, they've limited their ability to reinvest in the bakery. This explains why the business has struggled to grow.

Step 2: Set a Reinvestment Goal

They decide to set aside 10% of the bakery's profits each month for reinvestment. This will help them upgrade their equipment, hire extra help, or improve marketing - all things that will help the business grow. They also agree to limit the amount they withdraw from the business for personal expenses.

Step 3: Budget for Both Family and Business

With clearer boundaries between business and personal finances, they create two budgets: one for their family and one for the bakery. This helps them see exactly where their money is going and ensures that both their family and business are getting what they need.

Their Budget at a Glance:
- **Business Income:** £6,000 (monthly average)
- **Reinvestment:** £600 (10% of profits)
- **Personal Withdrawal:** £3,000 (to cover family expenses)
- **Remaining for Business Expenses:** £2,400 (for supplies, staff, etc.)

Reflection:

By setting boundaries between personal and business finances, Carlos and Maria feel more in control than ever. They're reinvesting in the bakery while still providing for their family, ensuring that neither side is sacrificed. This newfound clarity allows them to make decisions with confidence, knowing that each pound has a purpose. By protecting their business from personal expenses, they are laying the groundwork for both long-term growth and family security. This balance brings them peace of mind, turning what was once a cycle of stress into a path toward stability.

Why a Budget Works

Each of these families has created a budget that works for them. Whether it's the Johnsons striking a balance, Lisa breaking free from the payslip-to-payslip cycle, the Martins saving for their future goals, or the Castillos finally separating personal and business finances, their budgets serve as their guiding roadmap. A budget isn't about restricting yourself; it's about gaining **clarity and control** over your money.

A well-crafted budget offers freedom: the freedom **to focus** on what truly matters, to save for long-term goals, and to reduce the stress caused by financial uncertainty. It provides a structure to help you move from chaos to control, allowing you to prioritize what's most important without feeling lost. The clarity a budget brings doesn't limit you; it empowers you to make informed decisions, embrace opportunities, and face challenges with confidence. By aligning spending with your goals, you gain the peace of mind to navigate both everyday needs and future aspirations.

Ultimately, a budget is your most powerful tool for transforming financial disorder into a clear, **actionable plan for success**.

Next Steps: Tracking and Adjusting Your Budget

Now that these families have created their budgets, the next step is to track their spending and make adjustments along the way. In the next chapter, we'll guide them (and you) through the process of tracking expenses, making sure the budget is realistic, and adjusting it as life changes.

Whether you're just starting out or fine-tuning your finances, tracking your spending is the key to making your budget work in the long run.

Reflection Questions:

What's one area of your spending that you tend to underestimate? How could tracking help you get a clearer picture of where your money is really going?

Are you setting aside enough for savings each month, or do you feel like there's no progress anyhow? What could you adjust to see more growth in your savings?

Do you have a "fun money" category in your budget, or does spending on enjoyment feel like a guilty pleasure? How could setting aside a specific amount for fun help you enjoy life without the stress of overspending?

If you own a business, are you clearly separating business and personal finances? How might setting clearer boundaries help both your business and your family thrive?

How does your current financial situation align with your long-term goals? Are there adjustments you can make in your budget to better support those goals?

Real-Life Reflection:

In reality, life is often more complicated than the examples in this book. We're not just managing one financial scenario, we're juggling many at once. This is why finances can feel overwhelming. But here's the thing: we already do this in other areas of life, even when it's hard. We make sure the kids get to school because we know it's crucial for their future. We shop for groceries even when we're short on time because it's a necessity. We catch that early train because we know our income depends on it.

We already handle tough responsibilities every day, so managing our money with the same structure is possible, it just requires a shift in how we view budgeting. A budget isn't a burden; it's a tool that helps us make sense of the chaos, just like these other commitments we already juggle.

The world is going through massive changes. In the next 10 years, the economy may shift in ways we've never seen before, and losing control now could make it harder to adapt. Decades ago, change felt slow, but today, it's accelerating. In the 90s, experts warned that the world could look different in 20 years. Now, in just 10 years, it will be hard to recognize the world we know.

Having a budget and feeling financially in control won't just help us survive these changes, it will help us thrive. It gives us clarity, keeps us mentally grounded, and allows us to live without constantly worrying about what tomorrow will bring. In uncertain times, **a budget planning matters more than ever**, providing the clarity and control we need to navigate the future with confidence.

Use next blank space, if you need to write thoughts.

From Chaos to Control: Building a Balanced, Stress-Free Financial Life

Chapter 4: Tracking Expenses Without Stress

Creating a budget is an important first step, but to make sure it works, you need to track your spending. Tracking isn't about nit-picking every pound you spend - it's about understanding your habits and making sure your money is working for you. When you track your expenses, you can see what's going well, where you might be overspending, and whether your budget needs tweaking.

In this chapter, we'll follow our four families as they begin to track their expenses and learn how small changes can make a big difference in sticking to their budgets.

The Johnson Family: Tracking to Balance Spending and Saving

For Sarah and James, tracking their expenses is about creating balance. They've built a budget that allows them to save while still enjoying small treats, but they know they need to make sure they're sticking to it. Tracking their spending helps them understand where their money is really going, especially when it comes to impulse purchases.

Step 1: Find a Tracking Method that Works

Sarah and James decide to use a simple budgeting app to track their expenses in real-time. The app connects to their bank accounts and categorizes their spending automatically, showing them exactly where they're spending the most.

After a few weeks of tracking, they notice that dining out is eating into their "fun money" category faster than expected. They hadn't realized how often they were ordering takeout on busy nights. By tracking these small purchases, they can make adjustments without feeling deprived.

Step 2: Make Adjustments

They decide to cut back on takeout by planning meals in advance and setting a specific "takeout night" once a week. This small change allows them to stay within their fun money limit while still enjoying dining out occasionally.

Reflection:

Tracking their expenses has helped Sarah and James see where they were overspending without feeling like they had to give up the things they enjoy.

It's not about restricting themselves; it's about finding balance and making their budget work for them.

A great tool for this is Lloyds Bank's Money Manager, available if you have an account. It offers a clear breakdown of all expenses, categorized right in your online banking page. Just seeing where your money is going, whether on groceries or entertainment, provides an easy, visual way to start gaining control. Other banks offer similar features, so you may already have access to this clarity. By tracking their spending this way, Sarah and James can spot the patterns and make more intentional choices without feeling deprived.

It's about being aware and making adjustments where it matters most, without sacrificing the things that bring joy and comfort into your life.

The Walker Family: Tracking to Break Free from Pay cheque-to-Pay cheque

Lisa Walker is focused on breaking free from the payslip-to-payslip cycle, and tracking her expenses is a crucial part of that process. By understanding exactly where her money is going, she can find small ways to free up cash for savings.

Step 1: Use a Simple Tracking System

Lisa opts for a simple spreadsheet where she lists all her income and expenses each week. She manually tracks her spending on groceries, childcare, utilities, and personal expenses, and color-codes her spreadsheet to see where she's spending the most.

After a few weeks of tracking, Lisa notices that her grocery bill is higher than she realized. She's been buying convenience foods to save time after long workdays, but those small purchases are adding up. By tracking her spending, she can see that meal planning and cooking in bulk could save her money.

Step 2: Adjust Spending Habits

Lisa decides to cut back on convenience foods by meal planning and shopping for groceries on sale. She also starts making larger batches of meals on weekends to reduce the temptation of buying takeout during the week. These small changes free up an extra £20-£30 each month, which she can now add to her emergency fund.

Reflection:

Tracking her expenses has opened Lisa's eyes to where even small adjustments can make a significant difference. She's realized that by tweaking a few spending habits, she can free up a little extra money each month. This has allowed her to start saving more regularly and feel a growing sense of relief when it comes to handling unexpected ones. With every small change, Lisa is gaining confidence. She no longer feels trapped in her finances but empowered, knowing that she's making steady progress toward building her financial cushion.

The Martin Family: Tracking to Save for Big Goals

For Chloe and David Martin, tracking their expenses is essential to keeping their big dream of starting a tech business on track. They've created a budget that separates personal and business savings, but now they need to ensure they're not overspending in their personal lives.

Step 1: Automating Tracking

Chloe and David use a budgeting app to track their expenses automatically. The app breaks down their spending into categories - housing, utilities, groceries, and entertainment - and gives them a snapshot of how much they've spent compared to their budget for the month.

After a few weeks of tracking, they realize they've been spending more on social activities than they expected. While they've been doing a good job saving for their business, their personal spending is higher than planned. Tracking shows them exactly where they need to make adjustments to stay on track with their goals.

Step 2: Adjust Social Spending

To stay on track, Chloe and David decide to limit their nights out and opt for more cost-effective ways to socialize with friends, like hosting game nights at home or exploring free events in their city. These small changes allow them to save more for their business while still enjoying time with friends.

Reflection:
Tracking their expenses has been a game-changer for Chloe and David, helping them align their spending with their long-term goals. By making small, intentional changes to their social spending, they've been able to keep their business savings on track while still enjoying their personal life.

They've discovered that prioritizing what truly matters, like their dream business, doesn't mean giving up everything else. It's about balance. Each time they see their savings grow, they feel more empowered, knowing that their choices today are paving the way for future success. It's this thoughtful approach that's allowing them to build a solid financial foundation while maintaining the freedom to enjoy the present.

By taking the time to track and reflect, they've realized that even small adjustments can bring clarity and control, making both their business dreams and personal fulfilment possible.

The Castillo Family: Tracking to Balance Business and Personal Finances

For Carlos and Maria Castillo, tracking their expenses is about ensuring that both their family and their bakery are financially stable. They've created two separate budgets, one for their personal finances and one for their business, but they need to track their spending closely to make sure they're not overspending in either area.

Step 1: Track Business and Personal Expenses Separately

Carlos and Maria start by using two tracking systems, one for their family's personal expenses and one for their bakery. For their personal expenses, they use a simple app that categorizes their spending. For their business, they use accounting software that tracks all their bakery's expenses and income.

After a month of tracking, they realize they've been dipping into their personal funds to cover some small business expenses. The bakery is doing well, but unexpected costs, like equipment repairs and additional supplies, have forced them to use personal savings to keep the business running smoothly.

Step 2: Adjust Their Reinvestment Plan

Carlos and Maria decide to increase the amount they set aside for reinvestment in the bakery each month. This gives them more flexibility to cover unexpected business expenses without dipping into personal funds.

By tracking both their personal and business expenses separately, they're able to see exactly where the money is going and make adjustments as needed.

Reflection:

Tracking their business and personal expenses separately has given Carlos and Maria a newfound sense of clarity. They've created strong boundaries between their finances, allowing them to see exactly where their money is going. This separation has given them greater confidence in managing both their family's financial stability and the growth of their bakery.

Now, they no longer feel overwhelmed by mixed finances, and they can focus on making deliberate decisions. With clearer goals and structure, they feel more in control of their future, ensuring that neither the family nor the business is neglected.

Simple Ways to Track Expenses

Tracking doesn't have to be complicated or time-consuming. Here are some simple methods that you can use to track your expenses, based on what works best for your family:

Budgeting Apps: There are many apps available that can track your expenses automatically by linking to your bank account. Apps like Mint, YNAB (You Need a Budget), or EveryDollar are great options for families who want a hands-off approach to tracking.

Spreadsheets: If you prefer a more manual method, using a simple spreadsheet can help you stay organized. List your income and expenses and update the spreadsheet weekly or monthly to see how you're doing.

The Envelope System: For those who prefer dealing in cash, the envelope system is a classic way to track spending. Set aside cash for each spending category (groceries, entertainment, bills, etc.) in separate envelopes, and once the money is gone, it's gone. This visual system can help you stay on track.

Expense Journals: For those who like writing things down, keeping a journal of your daily spending can help you stay mindful of where your money is going. At the end of each week, you can review your entries and make adjustments as needed.

Adjusting Your Budget Over Time

Tracking your expenses isn't just about seeing where your money is going - it's about making adjustments when needed.

Life changes, and so do your financial needs. Whether it's an unexpected medical bill, a job change, or a new savings goal, your budget should be flexible enough to adapt.

Here are a few reasons you might need to adjust your budget:

Unexpected Expenses: If a large, unexpected expense comes up, like a car repair or a medical bill, you may need to temporarily adjust your budget to cover it.

Income Changes: If your income increases or decreases, make sure your budget reflects those changes. Use extra income to increase your savings or pay down debt faster, and if your income drops, look for areas to cut back temporarily.

New Goals: As your financial situation improves, you might want to set new goals, like increasing your savings, paying off debt more aggressively, or investing in a business.

The key is to be flexible and make adjustments as needed without feeling like you've failed. A good budget is always evolving to meet your current needs.

Next Steps: Staying Consistent and Celebrating Wins

Now that these families are tracking their expenses, the next step is staying consistent and celebrating their progress along the way. Tracking isn't just about finding problems - it's about recognizing wins, no matter how small, and staying motivated.

Tracking expenses is about more than just identifying where things go wrong—it's about staying consistent and celebrating the small wins along the way. As these families begin tracking, they're discovering that progress isn't always about drastic changes. Sometimes, it's the little things: identifying areas where they're overspending, spotting harmless expenses that quietly add up, and using regular budget check-ins to stay on course. By doing this, they not only stay motivated but also align their spending with their goals, helping them achieve success faster and with more clarity.

Chapter 5: Paying Off Debt - The Smart Way

Debt can feel like a heavy weight that holds you back from financial freedom. For many families, it's not just the amount of debt that's overwhelming - it's figuring out how to tackle it while balancing all of life's other expenses. But here's the good news: paying off debt doesn't have to be overwhelming, and it can be done in a way that feels empowering and rewarding.

In this chapter, we'll follow our four families as they take steps to tackle their debt head-on. Whether it's credit card debt, loans, or other forms of borrowing, the key is to find a strategy that works for your situation - and stick to it. By choosing a method and taking consistent action, you'll start to see progress, and that progress will keep you motivated.

The Johnson Family: Using the Snowball Method for Quick Wins

For Sarah and James, debt is a constant source of frustration. They've been trying to pay off their credit card, car loan, and a small personal loan, but it feels like they're barely making progress. After creating their budget and tracking their spending, they're ready to focus on paying off their debt, and they've chosen the **snowball method** to get started.

What is the Snowball Method?

The snowball method involves paying off your smallest debt first, while continuing to make minimum payments on all your other debts. Once the smallest debt is paid off, you move on to the next smallest, and so on. This approach helps build momentum by giving you quick wins that keep you motivated.

Step 1: List All Debts from Smallest to Largest

Sarah and James make a list of all their debts:

- Credit card: £1,200
- Car loan: £5,000
- Personal loan: £8,500

They decide to focus on paying off the credit card first, while making minimum payments on the car loan and personal loan.

Step 2: Make Extra Payments on the Smallest Debt

By cutting back on their dining out expenses, they've freed up £100 a month, which they put toward their credit card. With each extra payment, they watch the balance shrink, and after a few months, the credit card is paid off.

Step 3: Move to the Next Debt

Once the credit card is paid off, they move on to the car loan, putting the money they were using for the credit card toward the car loan instead. With each debt they pay off, they feel more confident and less burdened.

Reflection:

The snowball method works well for Sarah and James because it gives them quick wins and keeps them motivated. Paying off the smallest debt first helps them see progress, which encourages them to keep going.

The Walker Family: Tackling Debt with the Avalanche Method

For Lisa Walker, the focus is on reducing her credit card debt, which has been growing steadily due to unexpected expenses and high-interest rates. After tracking her spending and freeing up some money in her budget, Lisa has decided to use the **avalanche method** to tackle her debt.

What is the Avalanche Method?

The avalanche method focuses on paying off the debt with the highest interest rate first. This method saves you the most money in the long run, because you reduce the amount of interest you're paying. It's a slower start than the snowball method, but it's more efficient over time.

Step 1: List All Debts by Interest Rate

Lisa lists her debts in order of interest rates:

- Credit card: £1,800 (18% interest)
- Medical bill: £900 (5% interest)
- Personal loan: £2,400 (3% interest)

She decides to focus on paying off the credit card first since it has the highest interest rate.

Step 2: Make Extra Payments on the Highest-Interest Debt

By reducing her grocery bill and canceling unnecessary subscriptions, Lisa is able to free up £40 a month. She puts this extra money toward her credit card while continuing to make minimum payments on her other debts.

Step 3: Move to the Next Debt

Once her credit card is paid off, Lisa moves on to the medical bill, putting the extra £40 a month toward it. This approach saves her hundreds in interest over time, even if it feels like slower progress in the beginning.

Reflection:

The avalanche method is perfect for Lisa because it minimizes the interest she's paying. While it might feel slower at first, the long-term benefits are worth it, as she'll save more money and pay off her debt faster overall.

The Martin Family: Tackling Debt While Saving for a Dream

Chloe and David Martin have a unique challenge - they're saving for their business while also trying to pay off debt. They want to be strategic, ensuring they reduce their debt without jeopardizing their savings goal. For them, a blended approach works best.

Step 1: Prioritize High-Interest Debt

Chloe and David decide to tackle their credit card first, as it has the highest interest rate. They use the avalanche method to pay this off while making minimum payments on their other debts.

Step 2: Balance Debt Repayment and Savings

At the same time, they set aside a fixed amount each month toward their business savings goal. They know that starting a business will require significant investment, so they want to ensure they're still building their savings while paying down their debt.

Step 3: Reevaluate as Debt Decreases

As they pay off their credit card, they gradually increase their business savings. Once the high-interest debt is paid off, they shift focus to more aggressive business savings, while continuing to pay down their lower-interest debts at a steady pace.

Reflection:

For Chloe and David, balancing debt repayment with saving for their business dream is essential. They understand that tackling their high-interest debt first will help them save money over time, but they don't want to sacrifice their long-term goal of starting a business. A blended approach allows them to strike that balance.

By using the **avalanche method**, they focus on paying off the debt with the highest interest rate first, minimizing the amount of interest paid overall. At the same time, they set aside a small percentage of their income for business savings, ensuring their dream stays within reach. This method lets them reduce debt efficiently while keeping their entrepreneurial vision alive.

This combination of **focused debt repayment** and **gradual savings** not only lowers financial stress but also provides motivation. Chloe and David see progress on both fronts, giving them confidence in their ability to manage both short-term financial health and long-term goals.

The Castillo Family: Managing Business and Personal Debt

Carlos and Maria Castillo face the challenge of managing both personal and business debt. They've been using business profits to cover personal expenses, and as a result, their debts have piled up on both fronts. Now, they're focused on separating their finances and tackling their debt strategically.

Step 1: Separate Business and Personal Debt

Carlos and Maria start by separating their business and personal debts. They list their personal debts (a credit card and a small personal loan) and their business debts (a loan for new equipment). This clarity helps them prioritize what needs to be paid off first.

Step 2: Focus on Business Reinvestment

They decide to prioritize paying off their business loan, as the bakery's profitability depends on reducing its debt burden. By paying off the equipment loan first, they free up more cash flow for reinvesting in the business.

Step 3: Create a Personal Debt Plan

At the same time, they commit to making steady payments on their personal debt. They use the snowball method for personal debts, paying off the smallest one first to keep themselves motivated.

Reflection:

For Carlos and Maria, separating their business and personal finances was crucial to managing their debt effectively. By focusing on the business first, they ensure its long-term success, while still making progress on their personal debts using the snowball method.

Choosing the Right Debt Repayment Strategy

Each family has chosen a debt repayment strategy that fits their specific needs:

The Johnsons used the snowball method to build momentum and stay motivated with quick wins.

Lisa Walker chose the avalanche method to reduce interest and pay off her debt faster.

Chloe and David Martin found a balance between debt repayment and saving for their dream business.

Carlos and Maria Castillo separated their business and personal debt, tackling their business debt first to ensure future growth.

The right debt repayment strategy depends on your goals and financial situation. If you're motivated by quick wins, the **snowball method** might work best for you. If you want to save the most money in the long run, the **avalanche method** could be the better choice.

Fun Activity: Debt Payoff Thermometer

Here's a fun way to stay motivated while paying off debt: create a Debt Payoff Thermometer. Draw a large thermometer and mark each section with a debt milestone (e.g., £500, £1,000, £5,000). As you pay off your debt, colour in each section of the thermometer to show your progress. This visual reminder will keep you motivated and help you celebrate every milestone along the way.

Reflection Questions:

Which debt repayment strategy (snowball or avalanche) makes the most sense for your situation? Why?

How much extra money can you put toward debt each month without feeling overwhelmed? Are there areas in your budget where you could free up some extra cash?

What are the emotional or mental benefits of paying off your smallest debt first? Would quick wins help you stay motivated, or are you more focused on reducing interest payments over time?

If you have both personal and business debts, how can you prioritize which to pay off first while ensuring both your family and your business remain financially stable?

Choosing the right debt repayment strategy depends on your personal situation, but both methods offer powerful ways to reduce debt and build financial freedom.

The most important thing is to take consistent steps toward paying off debt, no matter which strategy you choose.

What's Next? Building a Savings Cushion for the Future

Now that our families are on the path to paying off their debt, the next step is building a financial cushion for the future.

In the upcoming chapter, we'll explore the importance of saving, both for emergencies and for long-term goals. We'll help you create a savings plan that fits your lifestyle and financial goals, so you can start building a more secure future for yourself and your family.

Saving money doesn't have to be stressful, it can be empowering.

Chapter 6: Save More, Worry Less

Saving money is like building a savings cushion - even in small amounts - can make a world of difference. Having money set aside gives you peace of mind, knowing that you can handle life's surprise expenses and take steps toward your bigger financial goals.

In this chapter, we'll follow our four families as they learn to build consistent savings habits that align with their financial goals.

They'll explore different strategies, such as automating their savings to make it effortless and prioritizing smaller, achievable goals to build momentum. Along the way, they'll discover that saving isn't just about numbers, it's about mindset, consistency, and aligning today's actions with tomorrow's dreams.

The Johnson Family: Building an Emergency Fund

For Sarah and James Johnson, the biggest financial stress comes from unexpected expenses. Whether it's a car repair, a medical bill, or school fees for the kids, every time something unexpected happens, it wipes out their savings. They know they need to build an emergency fund, but saving always seems to take a back seat to more immediate needs.

Step 1: Set a Realistic Savings Goal

Sarah and James decide to start small. Instead of focusing on saving a huge amount all at once, they set a goal of saving £1,000 over the next six months. This gives them a realistic target to aim for, without feeling overwhelmed.

Step 2: Automate Savings

To make saving easier, they set up an automatic transfer of £150 a month into a separate savings account. By automating their savings, they're paying themselves first - before they have a chance to spend the money on other things.

Step 3: Build Slowly and Celebrate Progress

As the months go by, Sarah and James see their savings grow, and it motivates them to keep going.

They celebrate each small milestone - when they reach £500, they treat themselves a fun afternoon at a local park with outdoor activities. These rewards make the journey enjoyable and special, while keeping the focus on their bigger financial goals without breaking the bank.

Reflection:

For Sarah and James, automating their savings has been a game-changer. Without having to actively think about it, they've managed to steadily build their emergency fund while still enjoying their current lifestyle.

Knowing that a portion of their income is automatically set aside each month has reduced their stress and given them peace of mind.

They no longer feel guilty about spending on occasional treats because they're confident that their financial future is secured. This effortless approach has made them feel better prepared for life's whatever is to come, while maintaining a sort of balance.

The Walker Family: Creating a Safety Net on a Tight Budget

Lisa Walker, as a single mom, constantly worries about what would happen if she faced a big financial emergency. Whether it's a medical bill or a sudden job loss, the idea of not having a safety net keeps her up at night. But with her tight budget, finding money to save feels impossible.

Step 1: Start Small and Build Momentum

Lisa knows that saving £1,000 feels out of reach, so she sets a smaller goal: saving £20 from each pay cheque. It's a modest start, but it's enough to give her a sense of progress. By starting small, Lisa can slowly build momentum without feeling discouraged.

Step 2: Use Unexpected Income for Savings

Anytime Lisa gets a little extra money - whether it's from a tax refund, a work bonus, or selling unused items - she puts it directly into her savings account. These small windfalls help her grow her savings faster without cutting into her regular budget.

Step 3: Make Saving a Priority

Even though Lisa's budget is tight, she treats her savings like any other essential bill. Each month, she sets aside the £20 before paying for other non-essential expenses. By making saving a priority, she's slowly building an emergency fund that will help her handle further.

Reflection:

Lisa has discovered that even setting aside just £4 on most days can make a big difference. She might not manage to save every single day, but if she puts away £4 for most of the year, she could have over **£1,100** in her emergency fund by the end of 12 months. That's a significant cushion compared to having nothing at all. This gradual, consistent effort helps her feel more secure, knowing that she's taking steps toward financial stability, no matter how small they seem in the moment.

The Martin Family: Balancing Savings with Big Goals

Chloe and David Martin have big dreams of starting their tech business, but they also know they need a financial cushion to protect themselves from unexpected setbacks. They don't want to sacrifice their business savings, so they decide to create separate savings goals for emergencies and their business.

Step 1: Separate Business and Personal Savings

Chloe and David set up two separate savings accounts - one for their business and one for emergencies. This helps them see clearly how much they're saving for each goal and prevents them from dipping into their business fund when unexpected expenses arise.

Step 2: Automate Both Savings

They set up automatic transfers into both accounts. Each month, they transfer £200 into their business savings and £100 into their emergency fund. By automating these savings, they ensure that both goals are being worked toward consistently.

Step 3: Review and Adjust as Needed

As their income fluctuates, they periodically review their savings plan. If they have a particularly good month, they increase their savings for both accounts. If a large expense comes up, they make sure their emergency fund is there to cover it, keeping their business fund untouched.

Reflection:

By setting up separate savings accounts, Chloe and David have found a way to work toward their dream of starting a business while still ensuring they build a financial safety net. They no longer worry about mixing funds, which gives them confidence that if life throws a curveball, like an unexpected expense, they'll be ready to handle it without derailing their long-term goals. For instance, by saving £50 a week toward their business and £30 toward their emergency fund, they can steadily grow both without sacrificing one for the other, striking a perfect balance.

The Castillo Family: Saving to Reinvest in the Business

For Carlos and Maria Castillo, the biggest challenge is balancing the needs of their family with the demands of their bakery. They know they need to reinvest in their business to help it grow, but they also need to create a personal savings cushion in case of emergencies.

Step 1: Set Clear Reinvestment and Personal Savings Goals

Carlos and Maria decide to set aside 10% of the bakery's profits each month for reinvestment and another 5% for their personal savings. This way, they're saving for both their business and their family's future without sacrificing one for the other.

Step 2: Automate Savings for Both Goals

They set up two separate accounts - one for business reinvestment and one for personal savings. By automating the process, they ensure that a portion of their profits is going toward growth, while still protecting their family's financial security.

Step 3: Adjust as the Business Grows

As the bakery becomes more profitable, Carlos and Maria adjust their savings contributions. They increase their reinvestment in the business, knowing that growth will lead to higher future profits, and they also increase their personal savings as their income rises.

Reflection:

For the Castillos, finding the right balance between reinvesting in their bakery and building personal savings has been a game-changer.

By separating these two financial goals, they're ensuring the bakery has the resources it needs to grow while still creating a financial cushion for their family.

For example, they dedicate 20% of the bakery's monthly profits to reinvest in equipment or marketing, while setting aside 10% of their personal income for family savings.

This structure gives them peace of mind, knowing they're securing both their family's future and their business's success

How to Build an Emergency Fund

No matter your financial situation, having an emergency fund is key to reducing stress and feeling secure. Here's a simple three-step guide to building your own emergency fund:

Set a Realistic Goal: Aim to save at least £500 to £1,000 to start. This will give you a small cushion for unexpected expenses. Over time, work toward saving three to six months' worth of living expenses.

Automate Your Savings: Set up automatic transfers from your checking account to a separate savings account. This way, you're consistently saving money each month without even thinking about it.

Cut Back on Non-Essential Expenses: Look for small areas where you can cut back - whether it's skipping takeout once a week or canceling unused subscriptions. Redirect that money into your emergency fund.

Fun Activity: The Vacation Jar

Saving doesn't have to be just about emergencies, it can also be about creating special moments! Start a "Vacation Jar" or a "Family Treat Fund" where everyone contributes a small amount each week toward a fun family goal, like a vacation or a special outing.

This activity teaches children the value of saving while giving the family something exciting to look forward to. Even small contributions add up over time, reinforcing that saving isn't only for necessities but for enjoying life, too.

Teaching Children the Importance of Saving

Introducing children to the concept of saving early helps them develop crucial habits that will serve them throughout their lives. Activities like the Vacation Jar show them, through action, how small, consistent efforts lead to bigger rewards. It's about more than just putting money aside, it's about learning how to plan, set goals, and stick to them.

As they see their contributions grow, they begin to understand the importance of **strategy** and **delayed gratification**, valuable life skills that will prepare them for bigger financial responsibilities in the future.

What's Next? Cutting Costs Without Feeling the Pinch

Now that our families have started building their savings, the next step is finding ways to cut costs without sacrificing their quality of life. Saving money doesn't have to mean giving up the things you enjoy - it's about making smart choices that allow you to live well while keeping more of your income.

In the upcoming chapter, we'll explore practical tips and strategies for reducing household expenses, finding hidden savings, and cutting unnecessary costs, all while still enjoying life. We'll see how our families can make small adjustments that lead to big savings over time, without feeling deprived.

Cutting costs is about being mindful of where your money goes, finding smarter alternatives, and making small changes that add up.

With these strategies, you'll learn how to save more while still enjoying the things that matter most.

Chapter 7: Cutting Costs Without Feeling the Pinch

For many people, the idea of cutting costs can seem intimidating. No one wants to feel like they have to give up the things they enjoy or make drastic changes to their lifestyle. But cutting costs doesn't have to mean sacrificing everything you love. With a few small adjustments, you can find room in your budget to save more without feeling deprived.

In this chapter, we'll follow our four families as they find creative ways to cut back on expenses - whether it's reducing household bills, finding cheaper entertainment options, or eliminating unnecessary spending.

You'll discover how simple changes can add up to big savings over time, allowing you to keep more of your money while still enjoying life.

The Johnson Family: Finding Hidden Savings in Everyday Expenses

For Sarah and James Johnson, cutting costs means finding areas in their daily spending where they could save without drastically changing their lifestyle. After building their emergency fund, they want to focus on increasing their savings by making smart decisions about their day-to-day expenses.

Step 1: Review Subscriptions and Monthly Bills

The first step for Sarah and James is reviewing their monthly subscriptions. Between streaming services, meal delivery plans, and app subscriptions, they're surprised by how much they're spending. They decide to cancel one streaming service they rarely use and pause their meal delivery plan, freeing up an extra £40 a month.

Step 2: Plan Meals and Reduce Grocery Costs

Next, Sarah starts planning their meals more carefully. Instead of picking up takeout on busy nights, she meal preps on Sundays, making enough for the week. This not only reduces their grocery bill but also cuts back on their takeout expenses. By sticking to a shopping list and avoiding impulse buys, they save another £60 each month.

Step 3: Find Fun, Low-Cost Entertainment

Instead of spending money on expensive family outings, they look for free or low-cost activities, like visiting parks, going for hikes, or having movie nights at home. This allows them to have fun as a family without overspending.

Reflection:

By reviewing their subscriptions, meal planning, and choosing low-cost entertainment, Sarah and James save £400 a month, money they can now put into savings or other financial goals.

For others, with higher incomes, such adjustments can lead to even larger savings. In households with incomes of £4k to £6k a month, cutting unnecessary expenses can free up enough for a significant down payment on a buy-to-let property in as much as 3 years. It's remarkable how much potential we overlook when we don't structure our finances, and we let ourselves to throw money and slip away instead of putting it to work. Small changes today can create stability and a lasting wealth for tomorrow.

The Walker Family: Cutting Costs on a Tight Budget

Lisa Walker, as a single mom on a tight budget, has already made several sacrifices to make ends meet. But she's determined to find additional savings, even if they're small, to build her emergency fund faster and reduce her financial stress.

Step 1: Reduce Energy Costs

Lisa starts by cutting her energy bill. She begins unplugging appliances when they're not in use, using energy-efficient light bulbs, and turning down the heat by just a couple of degrees. These small changes save her around £35 a month on her energy bill.

Step 2: Embrace DIY Solutions

To cut back on personal expenses, Lisa decides to embrace DIY. Instead of paying for expensive haircuts, she trims her kids' hair at home. She also starts doing more DIY cleaning and home maintenance, which saves her from hiring professionals for minor tasks. These changes add up to another £45 in savings each month.

Step 3: Use Coupons and Sales for Groceries

Lisa becomes more mindful of using coupons and buying items on sale when shopping for groceries. By planning her meals around weekly sales and using loyalty programs at the supermarket, she reduces her grocery bill by £15 each month.

Reflection:

For Lisa, every little bit counts, and she's not alone in making changes, her husband is fully on board too. Together, they're cutting energy costs by turning off lights and appliances when not in use, embracing DIY solutions for small repairs, and using coupons for groceries.

These small adjustments add up to an extra £60 a month, giving them more breathing room in their budget. For example, by saving £30 on energy and £20 on DIY projects, they can now redirect that money toward savings or paying down debt, offering greater financial peace.

With DIY, it's not just about saving money, it's also rewarding. Every time Lisa and her husband take on a project themselves rather than paying a subcontractor, they immediately redirect that saved money into their savings account. Whether it's painting a room or fixing a leaky faucet, the satisfaction of completing the task themselves makes the effort worthwhile. Plus, knowing that each project brings them closer to their financial goals adds extra motivation. It feels better, both emotionally and financially, to see the results of their hard work.

The Martin Family: Cutting Costs While Saving for Big Goals

Chloe and David Martin are focused on saving for their tech business, but they know that cutting costs in their personal lives can help them reach their business goals faster.

They want to reduce unnecessary spending without feeling like they're giving up the things they enjoy.

Step 1: Evaluate Dining and Social Spending

Chloe and David realize that dining out with friends and attending social events have been eating into their budget.

They agree to limit dining out to once a week and invite friends over for dinner at home instead.

By cooking for themselves and hosting game nights or movie marathons, they save around £230 a month.

Step 2: Negotiate Bills

David takes the time to call their internet provider and negotiates a lower rate for their plan. He also shops around for better car insurance and finds a deal that saves them £45 a month. These small negotiations reduce their monthly bills without sacrificing the quality of their services.

Step 3: Reevaluate Gym Memberships and Hobbies

Chloe cancels her rarely used gym membership and starts running outside and doing home workouts instead. David finds free online tutorials for his hobby of learning a new language, saving them £30 a month in total.

Reflection:

By making small adjustments to their dining and social habits, negotiating bills, and tweaking their hobbies, Chloe and David have managed to cut £150 a month from their expenses.

This extra cash is now being funnelled directly into their business savings fund, giving them a sense of progress toward their dream. For example, by opting for home-cooked meals instead of dining out and replacing expensive hobbies with low-cost alternatives, they're gradually building up the capital needed for their startup. Each month, they feel more in control and motivated, knowing these changes are fuelling their future success.

The Castillo Family: Saving While Running a Business

Carlos and Maria Castillo, who run a family bakery, are always looking for ways to reinvest in their business, but they know they need to cut personal and business expenses to make that possible. Their goal is to reduce unnecessary spending and increase profitability.

Step 1: Reduce Business Waste

Carlos and Maria look at their bakery's inventory and realize they're wasting more ingredients than they should be. They adjust their ordering to match actual sales and use leftover ingredients creatively in new recipes. This small change reduces waste and saves them around £75 a month in business costs.

Step 2: Review Personal Spending

On the personal side, Maria reviews their family's grocery bill and starts buying in bulk for items they use regularly, which reduces their overall food costs. She also cuts back on personal luxury purchases, like coffee shop visits, and makes coffee at home instead, saving them £40 a month.

Step 3: Combine Business and Family Resources

They also find ways to combine their business and personal resources. For example, they use leftover bakery supplies for family meals, which helps them reduce grocery expenses further.

Reflection:

By reducing business waste, adjusting personal spending, and finding ways to be more resourceful, Carlos and Maria now save £115 each month.

This extra money allows them to reinvest more into their bakery, purchasing better supplies or upgrading equipment, while also boosting their personal savings. For example, by minimizing food waste in the bakery and cutting unnecessary household expenses, they can steadily grow their financial cushion.

These small, intentional changes are creating a dual benefit: strengthening both their business and their personal finances, making their goals feel more achievable.

Practical Tips for Cutting Costs Without Feeling the Pinch

Here are some easy ways to cut costs while still enjoying your life:

Review Your Subscriptions: Cancel or pause any subscriptions or memberships you no longer use regularly. Services like streaming platforms, meal kits, or premium apps can add up quickly if they're not being used.

Meal Planning: Plan your meals for the week and stick to a shopping list when you go grocery shopping. This helps avoid impulse purchases and cuts down on food waste.

Cut Back on Dining Out: Limit how often you dine out and try cooking more meals at home. If you enjoy dining out, set a specific budget or limit it to once a week as a treat.

Use Coupons and Loyalty Programs: Look for discounts, coupons, or loyalty programs at your favorite stores. These small savings can add up over time, especially on regular purchases like groceries.

Negotiate Your Bills: Call your service providers (internet, phone, insurance) and ask for better rates. Sometimes simply asking can result in lower bills.

Unplug and Save on Energy Bills: Turn off lights, unplug appliances when not in use, and consider switching to energy-efficient appliances to reduce your utility costs.

Fun Family Challenge: The No-Spend Weekend

Here's a fun way to cut costs: try a **No-Spend Weekend** with your family.

The goal is to go an entire weekend without spending any money on non-essential items. Instead, focus on free activities like hiking, having a picnic, or playing games at home.

At the end of the weekend, see how much you saved and put that money toward a family goal - whether it's saving for a vacation or boosting your emergency fund.

Reflection Questions:

What's one area of your spending where you think you could cut back without feeling deprived? How could tracking help you identify these areas?

Do you have any subscriptions, memberships, or monthly services that you don't use as often as you thought? How much could you save by canceling or pausing them?

Could meal planning or cutting back on dining out help you reduce your grocery or entertainment costs?

Are there any bills or services you could negotiate for a better rate? What's stopping you from calling your providers to ask?

What's Next? Planning for the Future: Kids & Money

Now that our families have learned how to cut costs and save more, it's time to think about the future - especially when it comes to teaching our children about money.

In the next chapter, we'll explore how to introduce money concepts to children, helping them develop good financial habits from a young age.

We'll guide our families (and you) through practical, engaging ways to teach kids about budgeting, saving, and spending wisely, skills that set them up for long-term financial success. Whether you have young children or teenagers, it's never too early or too late to start showing them how to manage money effectively.

I won't go into why this is important, because you already understand that. Instead, we'll focus on **how** you can make these lessons part of everyday life, helping your children build healthy financial habits.

Chapter 8: Planning for the Future: Kids & Money

One of the most important lessons you can teach your children is how to manage money wisely. Whether they're earning an allowance or saving for something they want, learning about money early on helps them develop good financial habits that will serve them throughout their lives.

The sooner children will understand the basics of budgeting, saving, and spending, the better equipped they'll be to make smart financial decisions as they grow.

In this chapter, we'll explore fun and simple ways to introduce kids to key money concepts and help them build a strong financial foundation.

From creating hands-on activities like saving jars to teaching them how to budget their allowance, these methods are designed to make learning about money engaging and interactive. You'll discover how to incorporate lessons about saving, spending, and even goal setting into everyday life, helping your children develop healthy financial habits that will set them up for future success.

The Johnson Family: Teaching Kids About Budgeting with Allowances

For the Johnsons, teaching their children, Max and Emily, about money has become a priority. Sarah and James want to make sure their kids understand how to manage an allowance and make thoughtful spending decisions. They decide to set up an allowance system to give the kids hands-on experience managing their own money.

Step 1: Set Up an Allowance System

Sarah and James agree to give Max and Emily a weekly allowance based on their ages and responsibilities around the house. For example, Max, who is older, receives £25 a week, while Emily gets £17. The children are responsible for using their allowance for personal spending on toys, treats, or saving for something bigger.

Step 2: Teach the Basics of Budgeting

They teach the kids to divide their allowance into three categories: **Saving**, **Spending**, and **Giving**. Each child sets aside a portion of their allowance for short-term spending, saving for future goals (like a new toy), and donating to a cause they care about.

While not everyone may choose to donate to charity, it can be a valuable lesson in empathy and sharing. The goal is to teach kids how to manage money.

Step 3: Encourage Goal Setting

Max wants to save for a video game, while Emily is eyeing a new art set. Sarah and James encourage them to set specific savings goals and track their progress over time. Seeing their savings grow motivates them to stick with their budgets and make thoughtful spending decisions.

Reflection:

By setting up an allowance system and teaching budgeting basics, Sarah and James are laying a strong foundation for Max and Emily's financial future.

Each week, the children learn to allocate their money into different categories, spending, saving, and even giving, helping them understand the value of every penny. These small, practical lessons are building not only their confidence in managing money but also fostering a sense of responsibility.

As they grow older, these skills will become second nature, preparing them for larger financial decisions, from saving for a car to managing a pay cheque or a student loan. These early habits are vital stepping stones for financial independence and success in adulthood.

The Walker Family: Saving for the Future on a Tight Budget

As a single mom, Lisa Walker wants to ensure her kids, Jake and Chloe, understand the value of money, even though their budget is tight. She introduces the three-jar method to teach them how to balance spending, saving, and giving.

Step 1: The Three-Jar Method

Lisa provides each child with three jars: **Save**, **Spend**, and **Give**. Whenever they receive money, whether through small chores, birthday gifts, or allowances, they divide it between these jars.

The **Save** jar is for future goals, the **Spend** jar is for fun purchases, and the **Give** jar is for donations to causes they care about. Events like Yellow Day and Red Nose Day at their school give the children a chance to use their **Give** jar, allowing them to participate in charitable efforts in a balanced way.

This method teaches them not only the importance of managing money wisely but also instils a sense of social responsibility.

Step 2: Involve the Kids in Family Finances

Lisa also involves Jake and Chloe in small family budget discussions. When grocery shopping, she gives them a small budget and lets them choose what to buy. This helps them learn about making trade-offs and sticking to a budget.

Step 3: Teach the Importance of Saving

Chloe is saving up for a new bicycle, while Jake is putting money aside for a skateboard. Lisa encourages them to think long-term and teaches them that saving for big goals requires patience. Every time they add money to their "Save" jars, they get excited to see their progress.

Reflection:

Lisa's three-jar system is teaching Jake and Chloe valuable lessons about managing money wisely, even in a household with a tight budget.

By dividing their money into **Save**, **Spend**, and **Give** categories, they're learning that financial responsibility is key to achieving their goals.

This approach not only shows them how to balance short-term spending with long-term saving but also instils a sense of generosity through their contributions to school charity events.

The Martin Family: Introducing Money Concepts to Their Nephews

Chloe and David Martin don't have children yet, but they take the opportunity to teach their nephews, aged 8 and 14, about money management.

Every Sunday or during family gatherings, they talk to the boys about the importance of developing good financial habits early on.

Step 1: Teaching Through Real-Life Examples

When Chloe and David go grocery shopping or discuss big purchases, they use these moments to explain how they budget and save.

They highlight the importance of saving for future goals, like vacations or their tech business, to show the value of delayed gratification.

Step 2: Learning Through Conversations

Even though their nephews don't have allowances, Chloe and David encourage learning by engaging the boys in conversations about setting goals and saving for things they care about.

They believe these early lessons will help their nephews grow up with a clear understanding of managing money wisely.

Reflection:

By using real-life examples and open conversations, Chloe and David are laying the foundation for their nephews to build strong financial habits. They hope that these early discussions will help the boys save for their dreams and avoid years of missed opportunities.

The Castillo Family: Teaching Kids About Business Finances

Carlos and Maria Castillo, who run a family bakery, want to teach their kids about money by involving them in the business. Their goal is to help their children, Mateo and Sofia, understand the value of hard work, saving, and managing money through real-life experience.

Step 1: Involving Kids in the Family Business

Carlos and Maria decide to let Mateo and Sofia help with small tasks at the bakery, such as restocking shelves or handling simple transactions at the register. They pay their children a small wage for their work, which gives them a firsthand understanding of how hard work leads to earning money.

Step 2: Teaching Basic Business Concepts

At home, they introduce simple business concepts by explaining how the bakery makes money and how expenses like supplies and rent affect the family's income. This helps the kids see the connection between earning money and managing expenses.

Step 3: Encouraging Savings for Bigger Goals

Both Mateo and Sofia are encouraged to save part of their earnings for future goals, whether it's a new gadget or something more long-term like university.
Carlos and Maria teach them that saving is essential, not just for personal goals but also for growing the family business.

Reflection:

By involving their children, Mateo and Sofia, in the family business, Carlos and Maria are not only teaching them valuable lessons about work, money, and entrepreneurship, but also instilling a deep understanding of how finances are tied to effort and strategy. The hands-on experience of helping with the bakery gives them real-world skills, from budgeting to managing income, while also fostering a strong work ethic. These lessons won't just help Mateo and Sofia manage their personal finances, they're also preparing them for future responsibilities, whether they choose to stay in the family business or start their own ventures.

Through daily involvement, the children learn how every decision impacts both the business and family, showing them that financial discipline and planning lead to long-term success. This early exposure to entrepreneurship gives them a head start on understanding the complexities of running a business, allowing them to approach future financial challenges with confidence and insight. These are lessons that will benefit them for years to come, far beyond the bakery doors.

Fun Ways to Teach Kids About Money

Teaching kids about money doesn't have to be boring! The following are some fun, practical ways to make learning about money engaging for kids of all ages:

Allowance Systems: Give your kids an allowance based on their age or household chores. Teach them to divide it into categories for saving, spending, and giving.

Three-Jar Method: Use physical jars (or digital versions) to help kids divide their money into saving, spending, and donating. This visual method helps them understand the importance of budgeting for different needs.

Money Games: Use board games like **Monopoly** or online apps that teach basic money skills, such as saving, budgeting, and managing expenses in a fun, interactive way.

Involve Them in Budgeting: When shopping for groceries or planning a family vacation, give your kids a small budget to manage. Let them make decisions and understand how money is spent.

Goal Setting: Help your kids set specific savings goals and track their progress. Whether it's saving for a toy or a future trip, teaching them to work toward a goal helps them understand delayed gratification.

Fun Family Challenge: The Savings Jar Challenge

Create a savings jar for each family member and set specific goals for what you're saving for.

It could be something simple like a new toy or a family vacation. Every time someone adds money to their jar, celebrate the progress.

This teaches kids that small savings can add up over time and gives them a visual way to see how their efforts are paying off.

Reflection Questions:

How are you currently teaching your kids about money? What's one new method you could try to make it more engaging?

Are your children involved in your family's budgeting or spending decisions? How might giving them a small role help them learn more about managing money?

How could setting savings goals, even for young kids, teach them the importance of planning for the future?

Do you have a system in place for dividing your kids' money into saving, spending, and giving? How might this help them better manage their allowance or earnings?

Now that our families are teaching their kids about money, the next step is staying consistent. Financial success doesn't happen overnight - it's a journey that requires regular check-ins, small adjustments, and celebrating progress along the way.

In the next chapter, we'll focus on maintaining financial control by embracing progress over perfection.

We'll guide our families (and you) through setting financial milestones, adjusting budgets as needed, and staying motivated, even when things don't go as planned.

Financial control is about making steady progress, not aiming for perfection.

Chapter 9: Staying on Track: Progress, Not Perfection

Managing your finances is a lot like running a marathon, it requires persistence, consistency, and a willingness to make adjustments along the way. There will be bumps, and life will throw a lot your way, but that doesn't mean you've failed or that you will fail.

The key to long-term financial success is focusing on progress, not perfection.

Even small steps forward can lead to big changes over time. In this chapter, we'll follow our four families as they navigate the ups and downs of their financial journeys. We'll explore how they stay motivated, how they adjusted their plans, and celebrated their wins, no matter how small.

The Johnson Family: Embracing Progress Over Perfection

Sarah and James Johnson have been working hard to stick to their budget and save for their future, but it hasn't always been smooth sailing.

Unexpected expenses, like car repairs and school fees, have occasionally derailed their progress. However, instead of feeling discouraged, they've learned to focus on what they're doing right and adjust their plan when needed.

Step 1: Acknowledge Setbacks Without Guilt

When their car broke down unexpectedly, the repair bill wiped out a large chunk of their emergency fund. Initially, Sarah felt frustrated, thinking that all their hard work had gone to waste. But James reminded her that this was exactly why they'd built the emergency fund, to handle situations like this without going into another debt.

Step 2: Adjust the Plan

After using part of their emergency fund for a car repair, Sarah and James sit down to adjust their budget. They decide to temporarily increase their savings contributions to rebuild the fund, while cutting back on non-essential expenses like dining out.

However, they find a way to still enjoy life and each other, choosing to share a quiet bottle of wine at home after the kids go to bed.

These small moments of connection not only helped them save but also brought joy into their routine, proving that you don't have to sacrifice enjoyment while working toward your goals.

Step 3: Celebrate the Wins

Even though the car repair was a setback, they celebrate the fact that they didn't have to rely on credit cards or loans to cover the cost. This win keeps them motivated, and they remind themselves that their financial journey is about making steady progress, not achieving perfection.

Reflection:

For the Johnsons, setbacks no longer feel like reasons to give up. They've learned to focus on the progress they've made, like the fact that they had an emergency fund to tap into in the first place and adjust their plans as life unfolds. Instead of seeing challenges as failures, they now view them as opportunities to reassess and strengthen their strategy. Their ability to adapt gives them confidence that they're moving in the right direction, even when the road gets bumpy.

The Walker Family: Staying Consistent on a Tight Budget

As a single mom with a tight budget, Lisa Walker faces constant challenges. There are months when unexpected expenses throw off her carefully planned budget, and it feels like she's back to square one. But instead of giving up, Lisa has learned to stay consistent by focusing on small wins and making gradual improvements over time.

Step 1: Focus on Small Wins

Lisa sets realistic, short-term goals that keep her motivated. For example, even if she can only save £10 or £20 a month, she celebrates that win. Over time, these small savings add up, and Lisa in becoming more resilient and is able to gradually build her emergency fund.

Step 2: Adjust as Needed

When her children needed new school supplies, Lisa had to dip into her savings, but instead of feeling defeated, she adjusted her budget for the next month. She temporarily cut back on non-essential purchases and set a goal to rebuild her savings as soon as possible.

Step 3: Celebrate Progress, Not Perfection

Lisa understands that progress is more important than perfection. Each month, she checks in on her budget, celebrates the small victories - like staying under her grocery budget or avoiding impulse purchases - and adjusts where needed.

This keeps her motivated, even when money is tight.

Reflection:

For Lisa, staying consistent is key, but constantly cutting non-essential expenses can sometimes feel draining and stressful. Living on a tight budget often means sacrificing small pleasures, which can wear her down over time. However, she understands that these temporary sacrifices are part of a bigger picture. By focusing on small wins—like saving a little more each month—and adjusting her plan as needed, she's making steady progress toward her goals. While the journey is challenging, each step forward brings her closer to financial security, making the effort worthwhile.

After all, she did learn that staying consistent is key. She knows that building financial security takes time, but by focusing on small wins and adjusting her plan when needed, she's making steady progress toward her goals.

The Martin Family: Balancing Big Dreams with Day-to-Day Progress

Chloe and David Martin have big dreams of starting their tech business, but they also need to stay on top of their day-to-day finances. As they save for their business, they've learned to balance long-term goals with short-term progress, adjusting their plan when necessary.

Step 1: Set Milestones for Big Goals

Instead of getting overwhelmed by the amount they need to save for their business, Chloe and David break their goal down into smaller milestones. For example, their first goal is to save £5,000 for initial startup costs. Once they reach that milestone, they'll celebrate and move on to the next.

Step 2: Make Adjustments When Life Happens

When their heating system broke down, they had to use part of their savings to cover the cost. But instead of seeing this as a failure, they adjusted their savings plan and set a new timeline for their business goal. Life happens, and Chloe and David have learned to be flexible in their financial planning.

Step 3: Celebrate Progress Along the Way

Each time they reach a savings milestone, they celebrate their progress. Whether it's a dinner at home or a small treat, celebrating their wins keeps them motivated and reminds them that they're moving in the right direction.

Reflection:

For Chloe and David, staying on track requires balancing their long-term dreams with their immediate, day-to-day needs. By breaking their bigger goals into smaller, achievable milestones, they create a sense of steady progress.

Celebrating each small win, like hitting a savings target or paying off a bit of debt, helps them stay motivated, even when setbacks arise.

They've learned that reaching their dreams doesn't happen overnight, but by focusing on consistent effort and celebrating along the way, they maintain momentum and keep moving toward their goals with confidence and optimism.

The Castillo Family: Managing Business and Family Finances

Carlos and Maria Castillo juggle both personal and business finances, which means they're constantly adjusting their plan to keep everything running smoothly. They've learned that perfection isn't realistic, but steady progress keeps them on track.

Step 1: Regular Financial Check-Ins

Carlos and Maria set aside time every month to review both their personal and business finances. They look at what's working, where they might need to cut back, and how much they're able to reinvest in their bakery. These check-ins help them stay focused on their goals without feeling overwhelmed.

Step 2: Adjust When Business Is Slow

Running a business comes with its ups and downs, and there are months when sales are lower than expected. During slower months, Carlos and Maria adjust their personal spending to make sure they can still cover business expenses. They cut back on non-essentials and look for creative ways to increase sales, like offering special promotions at the bakery.

Step 3: Celebrate Personal and Business Wins

When the bakery has a great month or they reach a personal savings goal, Carlos and Maria make sure to celebrate. These celebrations, whether small or big, keep them motivated and remind them why they're working so hard to manage both their business and family finances.

Reflection:.

For Carlos and Maria, staying on track means finding a delicate balance between their personal and business finances. Running a small bakery comes with constant financial pressures, but through regular check-ins and honest discussions, they've learned to adapt their strategy when needed.

By reassessing their business and personal goals frequently, they can stay flexible, ensuring they're reinvesting in the bakery without neglecting their family's needs.

This balance has helped them manage the ups and downs of entrepreneurship while steadily moving toward financial stability for both their business and their family.

Fun Family Challenge: Monthly Financial Check-In

Set aside time each month for a Family Financial Check-In. During this time, review your budget, savings, and any financial goals you've set. Celebrate your wins, adjust your budget if necessary, and discuss any upcoming expenses or goals. Keep it fun by adding treats or rewards for reaching milestones, like a homemade dessert or a family movie night, or go out in Sunny Days.

Reflection Questions:

What financial setbacks have you faced recently? How did you adjust your plan to get back on track?

Do you regularly check in on your budget and financial goals? How could a monthly check-in help you stay consistent?

How do you celebrate your financial wins? What's one way you could reward yourself for reaching your next milestone?

Are there areas in your financial plan where you've been striving for perfection instead of focusing on progress? How could you adjust your mindset to embrace progress?

What's Next? Maintaining Control: Long-Term Success

Now that our families are staying consistent with their financial plans, it's time to think about the long term.

In the final chapter, we'll explore how to maintain financial control and build on the habits they've developed. We'll guide our families (and you) through strategies for ensuring their financial success continues well into the future - whether that's through retirement planning, investing, or long-term savings goals.

Financial success isn't just about reaching short-term goals; it's about building lasting habits that create security and freedom for the rest of your life.

Chapter 10: Maintaining Control and Long-Term Success

You've come a long way on your financial journey. From building a budget, cutting costs, paying off debt, and saving for the future, each step has brought you closer to financial freedom.

Now the challenge is maintaining control and keeping those positive habits going long-term. Financial success isn't just about reaching short-term goals - it's about making smart decisions that will serve you and your family well into the future.

In this chapter, we'll explore strategies to help our four families (and you) maintain financial control and continue building on the habits they've developed. Whether it's through retirement planning, investing, or managing long-term savings goals, these strategies will help ensure lasting financial security.

The Johnson Family: Preparing for Retirement and Long-Term Security

Now that Sarah and James Johnson have built an emergency fund, paid off some of their debt, and created a sustainable budget, their focus is shifting toward the long term. They want to make sure they're on track for retirement and that their family will be financially secure in the future.

Step 1: Boost Retirement Savings

Sarah and James both have access to workplace retirement plans but haven't contributed much beyond the minimum. Now that they've paid off some debt and are in a more stable position, they decide to increase contributions to 10% of their income. This takes full advantage of employer matching and ensures they're building a solid foundation for the future.

Step 2: Build Passive Income

Instead of relying on stocks and bonds, Sarah and James explore ways to generate passive income that they can control. They decide to rent out a spare room on platforms like Airbnb or offer services like tutoring and online workshops.

By creating multiple streams of income through skills they already have, they build a stronger financial buffer.

Step 3: Long-Term Savings for a Bigger Home

Sarah and James set a long-term goal of purchasing a larger home. To reach their target of **£85,000** for the down payment in **8 years,** they calculate they need to save **£885 per month**.

To stay on track, they set up a dedicated savings account and automate monthly contributions. By cutting non-essential expenses and sticking to this plan, they remain focused and motivated, ensuring that they are consistently working toward their goal while maintaining financial discipline.

Reflection:

By increasing their retirement contributions and focusing on practical passive income streams, such as renting out a room or offering skills-based services, Sarah and James are securing their financial future without relying on complex investments like stocks and bonds. Their passive income strategies allow them to generate extra cash flow while keeping things manageable. This approach, combined with their disciplined saving habits, helps them grow their finances steadily and build a stable future that they have control over, making financial security more tangible and attainable.

The Walker Family: Building Long-Term Stability on a Tight Budget

Lisa Walker has made incredible progress on her financial journey, building an emergency fund and sticking to her budget despite a tight income. Now, she's thinking about the future - how can she maintain her financial stability while preparing for major life events, like her children's education?

Step 1: Start a College Savings Fund

Even though Lisa's budget is tight, she knows it's important to start saving for her kids' future. She opens a savings account dedicated to her children's education and commits to contributing a small amount each month, even if it's just £20. Over time, these small contributions will grow, and she knows it will make a difference when it's time for her kids to go to university.

Step 2: Focus on Building Passive Income Over Time

While saving for her children's education, Lisa is thinking about ways to generate passive income alongside her regular job. She decides to use her creativity and resilience to start small ventures, like launching a YouTube channel where she crafts tiny cardboard houses for her children to decorate, involving them in the process. Additionally, as a nurse with extensive health knowledge, she begins writing health-related content and self-publishing her advice on Amazon.

Step 3: Plan for Future Financial Milestones

Lisa also sets specific goals, like paying off her car loan and eventually buying a home. She creates a timeline for these milestones, ensuring her budget allows for consistent savings toward them.

Reflection:

For Lisa, maintaining control means taking small, steady steps toward her long-term goals. By combining her passion for health and creativity, she's building passive income streams through YouTube and writing, while continuing her nursing career as her career is meaningful for her.

Over time, this additional income will help create financial stability, offering her greater flexibility and the freedom to pursue bigger dreams.

The Martin Family: Saving and Investing for Their Business and Future

Chloe and David Martin are balancing two major financial goals: saving for their tech business and planning for their personal future. Now that they've made progress toward their short-term savings goals, they're ready to think about how to grow their wealth and protect their long-term financial security.

Step 1: Invest in Their Business Growth

Chloe and David decide to reinvest part of their business savings into areas that can help it grow. They focus on upgrading their technology and expanding their staff, which allows them to scale the business. This reinvestment ensures long-term growth and stability.

Step 2: Create Passive Income

In addition to growing their business, Chloe and David look for passive income opportunities. They launch an online course based on their expertise and start selling digital products. This allows them to build wealth outside of their core business while diversifying their income streams.

Step 3: Focus on Financial Freedom

While Chloe and David are focused on growing their business, they also prioritize achieving financial freedom. Rather than thinking about traditional retirement, they aim to reach a point where they have enough passive income streams and savings to choose how and when they work. Their goal is to have the flexibility to pursue other passions or scale back their involvement in the business, all while maintaining a stable financial cushion. This mindset keeps them motivated to build wealth beyond just day-to-day business operations.

Reflection:

For Chloe and David, maintaining control is all about balancing their business growth with personal financial security.

By reinvesting in their company while building multiple streams of passive income, they're creating a sustainable foundation for the future.

Their focus on diversifying income sources, not just through traditional investments, ensures they're prepared for both personal and business success.

This holistic approach helps them achieve their long-term vision of financial freedom while still keeping their entrepreneurial spirit alive.

The Castillo Family: Maintaining Balance Between Business and Family Finances

Carlos and Maria Castillo have learned how to balance the needs of their family with the demands of running a bakery. Now, they're focused on maintaining that balance while planning for future growth in both their business and personal finances.

Step 1: Reinvest in the Business

Carlos and Maria continue reinvesting a portion of their bakery's profits to support growth. They purchase new equipment, expand their product offerings, and invest in marketing to attract new customers. This helps ensure the bakery's long-term success while providing a stable income for their family.

Step 2: Build Personal Savings

At the same time, they prioritize building their personal savings. They've already established an emergency fund, but now they focus on saving for other goals - like taking a family vacation and eventually purchasing a home. They automate monthly savings into separate accounts for each goal.

Step 3: Build a Team for Freedom

Chloe and David realized that to truly enjoy the fruits of their labour, they needed to step back from the daily grind. They started by hiring key employees, including a director of sales and marketing, which allowed the business to run efficiently without their constant involvement. This shift gave them the freedom to travel, visit family, and enjoy life more. By investing in their team, they've created a business that supports their personal lives, giving them the flexibility they've worked so hard to achieve.

Reflection:

For Chloe and David, maintaining control isn't about scaling their business to huge proportions but about growing it in a way that gives them balance.

By hiring employees and even a director of sales and marketing, they've built a strong team that allows the business to run smoothly without their constant oversight. This freedom gives them the chance to travel, visit family, and share the challenges of their entrepreneurial journey.

After years of focusing solely on earning wages, they can now enjoy life while knowing their business continues to thrive.

Key Strategies for Long-Term Financial Success

Reinvest in Growth: Whether it's investing in your business or in personal growth opportunities (like education or skill-building), reinvesting your profits helps ensure long-term success. Look for opportunities to improve your income sources and expand your financial potential.

Automate Savings and Investments: Automating your contributions to retirement accounts, savings accounts, or investments ensures that you're consistently building wealth. The more you automate, the easier it is to maintain good habits without thinking about it.

Plan for Major Milestones: Whether you're saving for a home, a child's education, or a dream vacation, setting clear financial milestones helps you stay on track. Create separate savings accounts for each goal and automate contributions to reach those milestones.

Review and Adjust Regularly: Life changes, and so should your financial plan. Review your finances regularly - whether it's annually or quarterly - and make adjustments based on your current situation and future goals.

Focus on Long-Term Security: Prioritize saving for retirement, building an emergency fund, and investing in assets that will grow over time. These steps will help ensure that you're financially secure, no matter what the future brings.

Fun Family Challenge: Future Goals Jar

Create a **Future Goals Jar** for your family. Each family member can write down a long-term goal they're saving for - whether it's a family vacation, a new home, or even a dream retirement.

Every month, contribute a little toward these goals and watch your savings grow. This visual reminder will keep everyone excited about reaching their long-term goals together.

Reflection Questions:

Are you currently contributing enough to your retirement savings? What steps can you take to increase those contributions?

Do you have long-term savings goals beyond retirement? What milestones are you working toward, and how can you adjust your budget to reach them faster?

How are you reinvesting in yourself, your family, or your business? What opportunities do you have to grow your income or skills over time?

When was the last time you reviewed your financial plan? How could a regular check-in help you stay on track?

From Chaos to Control: Building a Balanced, Stress-Free Financial Life

Throughout this book, we've followed the journeys of four families as they moved from financial chaos to control. From building budgets and cutting costs to saving for emergencies and long-term goals, each step has been part of a larger journey toward financial freedom.

Financial success doesn't happen overnight, but by making small, consistent improvements, you can build a solid foundation for yourself and your family. Remember, it's not about perfection - it's about progress. Celebrate the small wins, adjust your plan as needed, and stay focused on your long-term goals. You now have the tools and strategies to take control of your finances and create a more secure, stress-free future, even is for paying off debt, building savings, investing for the future, or teaching your kids about money, each step you take brings you closer to financial freedom.

Throughout this book, we've followed four families as they moved from chaos to control, tackling budgets, savings, and long-term goals. Financial success doesn't happen overnight, but consistent progress builds a solid foundation for your future.

In my opinion, the future will divide us into two groups: consumers and makers. Consumers are those who don't have a plan or they do but they don't action it, drifting through life like autumn leaves, never knowing where they're headed.

What is a fact is that if you don't keep track of your money, it'll disappear into someone else's hands.

Technology is shifting fast, and there are endless ways to step up as a maker, whether it's creating content or putting your skills to work. The key is to start thinking about savings, which most of us overlook. Saving gives us that feeling of safety, like the security of home. Unfortunately, savings is not something we naturally think about daily, but when we do, it changes everything.

We love the feeling of being safe, so why not create that safety with your money? Put some nets around it, protect it, and make your financial future secure. Keep your focus, stay consistent, and remember, progress, not perfection, will get you where you want to be.

From Chaos to Control: Building a Balanced, Stress-Free Financial Life

Table of Contents

Creating a Safety Net, Even When Times Are Tough, **PAGE 5**

Breaking the Cycle: You Can Do This

How to Find Room for Savings When There's "No Room"

The Long Game: Progress Over Perfection

You Deserve Financial Peace

Chapter 1: The Foundation, PAGE 14

The Johnson Family: Balancing Spending and Saving

The Walker Family: The Single Parent Balancing Act

The Martin Family: The Child-Free Couple with Big Dreams

The Castillo Family: The Family Business Under Stress

Why Reflecting on the Chaos Matters

What Being "Smart" with Money Really Means

Chapter 2: Starting with Chaos: Identifying the Problem, PAGE 31

The Johnson Family: Balancing Spending and Saving

The Walker Family: Breaking the Pay cheque to Pay cheque Cycle

The Martin Family: Bridging the Gap Between Dreams and Reality

The Castillo Family: The Struggle of Business and Personal Finances

Seeing the Bigger Picture: Why We Need a Plan

What`s Next? Creating a Roadmap for Success

Chapter 3: Building a Family Budget that Works, PAGE 45

The Johnson Family: Finding Balance Between Saving and Spending

The Walker Family: Breaking Free from Pay cheque-to-Pay cheque

The Martin Family: Saving for Big Dreams

The Castillo Family: Balancing Business and Family

Why a Budget Works

Chapter 4: Tracking Expenses Without Stress, PAGE 60

The Johnson Family: Tracking to Balance Spending and Saving

The Walker Family: Tracking to Break Free from Pay cheque-to-Pay cheque

The Martin Family: Tracking to Save for Big Goals

The Castillo Family: Tracking to Balance Business and Personal Finances

Simple Ways to Track Expenses

Adjusting Your Budget Over Time

Next Steps: Staying Consistent and Celebrating Wins

Chapter 5: Paying Off Debt – The Smart Way, PAGE 72

The Johnson Family: Using the Snowball Method for Quick Wins

The Walker Family: Tackling Debt with the Avalanche Method

The Martin Family: Tackling Debt While Saving for a Dream

The Castillo Family: Managing Business and Personal Debt

Choosing the Right Debt Repayment Strategy

Chapter 6: Save More, Worry Less, PAGE 84

The Johnson Family: Building an Emergency Fund

The Walker Family: Creating a Safety Net on a Tight Budget

The Martin Family: Balancing Savings with Big Goals

The Castillo Family: Saving to Reinvest in the Business

How to Build an Emergency Fund

Teaching Children the Importance of Saving

Chapter 7: Cutting Costs Without Feeling the Pinch, PAGE 96

The Johnson Family: Finding Hidden Savings in Everyday Expenses

The Walker Family: Cutting Costs on a Tight Budget
The Martin Family: Cutting Costs While Saving for Big Goals
The Castillo Family: Saving While Running a Business
Practical Tips for Cutting Costs Without Feeling the Pinch
Fun Family Challenge: The No-Spend Weekend

Chapter 8: Planning for the Future: Kids & Money, PAGE 110

The Johnson Family: Teaching Kids About Budgeting with Allowances
The Walker Family: Saving for the Future on a Tight Budget
The Martin Family: Introducing Money Concepts to Their Nephews
The Castillo Family: Teaching Kids About Business Finances
Fun Ways to Teach Kids About Money
Fun Family Challenge: The Savings Jar Challenge

Chapter 9: Staying on Track: Progress, Not Perfection, PAGE 122

The Johnson Family: Embracing Progress Over Perfection

The Walker Family: Staying Consistent on a Tight Budget

The Martin Family: Balancing Big Dreams with Day-to-Day Progress

The Castillo Family: The Castillo Family: Managing Business and Family Finances

Fun Family Challenge: Monthly Financial Check-In

Chapter 10: Maintaining Control and Long-Term Success, PAGE 133

The Johnson Family: Preparing for Retirement and Long-Term Security

The Walker Family: Building Long-Term Stability on a Tight Budget

The Martin Family: Saving and Investing for Their Business and Future

The Castillo Family: Maintaining Balance Between Business and Family Finances

Fun Family Challenge: Future Goals Jar

From Chaos to Control:

Building a Balanced, Stress-Free Financial Life

Continue Your Financial Journey with Money Prep Academy

At Money Prep Academy® Ltd, our mission is to help individuals and families take control of their finances and build a secure future. Our books are designed to provide simple, actionable advice that empowers you to make smart financial decisions and don't hesitate to reach out with questions or feedback. We're here to support you every step of the way.

Thank you for your time and for choosing Money Prep Academy®

www.moneyprepacademy.co.uk

One Penny at a time

About the Author

Alina Salabin is the founder and lead instructor at Money Prep Academy.

With a diverse professional background spanning law, finance, governance, risk management, and digital transformation, Alina is uniquely qualified to offer financial guidance rooted in real-world experience and best practices.

Alina holds qualifications in law and accounting, business, digital transformation and leadership. She worked as an accountant since 2015, provided tax advice since 2018, and has served as a Money Laundering Reporting Officer (MLRO) since 2020.

As a Fellow member of the ICA, FICA, International Compliance Association, Alina brings a wealth of experience to her work, and her passion for simplifying finance inspired the creation of Money Prep Academy.

Through Money Prep Academy, Alina's mission is to help individuals and families who may feel overwhelmed by finance by breaking down difficult concepts into simple steps.

Through her work, Alina aims to make simple most complex concepts about personal finance, enabling people to take control of their financial futures with confidence.

Money Prep Academy® Ltd Money Prep Academy is registered in England and Wales under CRN 15169086.

From Chaos to Control: Building a Balanced, Stress-Free Financial Life

www.ingramcontent.com/pod-product-compliance
Lightning Source LLC
Chambersburg PA
CBHW052202220526
45471CB00004B/1778